The First Great Awakening in
Colonial American Newspapers

The First Great Awakening in Colonial American Newspapers

A Shifting Story

Lisa Smith

LEXINGTON BOOKS
Lanham • Boulder • New York • Toronto • Plymouth, UK

Published by Lexington Books
A wholly owned subsidiary of
The Rowman & Littlefield Publishing Group, Inc.
4501 Forbes Boulevard, Suite 200, Lanham, Maryland 20706
www.rowman.com

10 Thornbury, Plymouth PL6 7PPw, United Kingdom

British Library Cataloguing in Publication Information Available

Library of Congress Cataloging-in-Publication Data

The hardback edition of this book was previously cataloged by the Library
of Congress:

Smith, Lisa, 1967-
  The first great awakening in colonial American newspapers : a shifting
story / Lisa Smith.
      p. cm.
  Includes bibliographical references and index.
  1. American newspapers—History—18th century. 2. Journalism—United
States—History—18th century. 3. Great Awakening. I. Title.
  PN4861.S65 2012
  071.3—dc23
                                                                    2011052292

ISBN: 978-0-7391-7274-2 (cloth : alk. paper)
ISBN: 978-0-7391-8824-8 (pbk. : alk. paper)
ISBN: 978-0-7391-7275-9 (electronic)

♾™ The paper used in this publication meets the minimum requirements of
American National Standard for Information Sciences—Permanence of
Paper for Printed Library Materials, ANSI/NISO Z39.48-1992.

Printed in the United States of America

Contents

List of Figures

Introduction

There is nothing more common than to judge of the Temper and Disposition of Men, or rather to settle the Character of an Age by its News Papers, which it must be owned is natural enough, since an Accumulation of Facts may be with some Colour stiled a History, and by the Lights afforded us by History, we are best enabled to judge of Men.

Boston Evening-Post, July 23, 1739[1]

"I therefore Warn you in Christ's Name, in Faithfulness to your Souls, To shun him as an open Enemy to Religion, whatever may be his specious Pretences, A Violator of all Rule and Order, disobeying those who have the Rule over him, and dispising [sic] his Betters. Don't suffer your selves to be imposed upon or drawn away by this Deceiver, but Watch and Pray that you enter not into Temptation." Thus ends a public denunciation of George Whitefield shortly after the English evangelist arrived for his first preaching tour of the American colonies in 1739. Written by Anglican clergyman Jonathan Arnold and printed in New York by William Bradford on November 17, 1739, Arnold's pamphlet "To the Inhabitants of New-York" provoked immediate response and generated a war of words in the newspapers that continued for three months and produced ten related newspaper articles.[2] Boston newspapers published the controversy, and the *Boston Weekly News-Letter* reprinted Arnold's original letter, causing Boston clergymen to debate the appropriateness of printing Arnold's derogatory comments. In Philadelphia, contributors to the *American Weekly Mercury*, writing under the pseudonyms "Magnus Falconar" and "Impartial Justice," criticized Arnold and defended Whitefield, forcing Arnold to defend himself in the *Mercury*. The *New-York Gazette* terminated the paper war with a two-page letter from Arnold and an anonymous poem satirically comparing Arnold to Sancho Panza, armor-bearer to the bungling hero Don Quixote. *Gazette* printer William Bradford noted that only "strong Importunity" made him print these last two contributions: "For the future we do not think to incert any more of these Controversies, not being proper for this Paper."

The paper war begun by Jonathan Arnold highlights the controversy and contention sparked by the religious events of the early 1740s, a movement historically referred to by scholars as the "First Great Awakening." Not since the time of the Half-Way Covenant in New England in 1662 had the colonies experienced more controversial, divisive, and stimulating religious events, and writings debating the movement and its key players were extensive. Colonial printers increased their percentage of religious works from more than 40 percent of total publications in 1738, one year before the movement began, to greater than 60 percent by 1741.[3] Historian Frank Lambert has observed that in 1745, the revival was the subject of 35 percent of all colonial publications and that 75 percent of all letters from Anglican clergymen in New England to the secretary of the Society for the Propagation of the Gospel in England during the years 1739-1745 had the revival as their subject.[4] Colonial printing in general in the colonies increased due to the excitement of the revival, with imprints almost doubling during 1740.[5]

Published sermons and pamphlets debating religious issues sparked by the revival were in constant demand, and reprintings of seventeenth-century Puritan writings became popular when revivalists recommended them.[6] Revivalist magazines such as George Whitefield's *Weekly History* in London, William Macculloch's *Glasgow Weekly History* in Scotland, and Thomas Prince, Jr.'s *Christian History* in Boston widely disseminated reports on the progress of the movement. Revival testimonies and Whitefield's journals recounting events from his personal spiritual life as well as his public ministry were widely disseminated. Even unpublished revival narratives and letters circulated throughout the colonies and beyond.

The printed record of the religious events in the 1740s has been studied by scholars since the nineteenth century, beginning with historian and clergyman Joseph Tracy. Tracy examined documents such as personal testimonies, published treatises, periodicals, and church records to present his history of the movement, which he termed the "Great Awakening." Scholars of the mid-twentieth century such as Edwin S. Gaustad, Alan Heimert, and Perry Miller studied sermons, pamphlets, and testimonies to evaluate the influence of the movement on later colonial developments such as the American Revolution.

More modern scholars have studied the printed works of the Awakening to identify the self-interest present in both contemporary and later accounts of the revival, leading some to question the historical accuracy of the movement as a whole. Historian Jon Butler was the first to offer this revisionist understanding of the movement by questioning Joseph Tracy's interpretation of events, claiming that Tracy's "interpretive fiction" convinced later scholars that the movement was genuine and far-reaching.[7] Joseph A. Conforti studied nineteenth-century interpretations of the Awakening, determining the revival to be a "cultural production" of these later revivalists to validate their own religious movement, the Second Great Awakening of the 1830s.[8] Frank Lambert used his study of eighteenth-century revival documents to assert that eighteenth-century revivalists themselves were responsible for creating the perception of revival, essentially "inventing" the Great Awakening through their use of print and oral media.[9]

Although recent scholars differ on the extent or influence of colonial events historically known as the Great Awakening, the extraordinarily widespread reporting of religious happenings during the early 1740s has been well-documented. This "little mountain of books and pamphlets," as James N. Green calls it,[10] at a minimum reveals that Christianity and the revivalists' innovative approach to religious practice were topics that the vast majority of colonists were aware of during those years, regardless of interpretation or whether such events can be labeled a "Great Awakening." Even those who disliked the incidents admitted that religion was the subject of the day and focused their publicity efforts on discrediting, not denying, the movement. The Rev. Charles Chauncy, one of the foremost eighteenth-century opponents of the Awakening in New England, admitted in his 1742 sermon

Enthusiasm Described and Cautioned Against (Boston, 1742), "There is, I doubt not, a great deal of real, substantial religion in the land. The Spirit of God has wro't effectually on the hearts of many, from one time to another. And I make no question he has done so of late, in more numerous instances, it may be, than usual."[11] The sheer amount of print devoted to religious activities in the 1740s constituted, in its own way, an "event" for American colonists.

One contemporary record of the religious events of the 1740s that has been examined only piecemeal is the account found in colonial American newspapers. Colonial newspapers covered the revival extensively and were one of the most significant means of transmitting information about the revival to the public. Historian Charles E. Clark remarks that American newspapers "more than any other single printed vehicle of the eighteenth century reflected the 'collective mentality' of the age."[12] Colonial newspapers provided for their readers the most expansive view available of colonial life and foreign affairs, and drew the scattered colonists into a network of shared communication and influence. American newspapers had been in existence about thirty years when the revival began, and fifteen English-language newspapers were publishing during the key years of the movement, located in the major colonial cities. Bostonians could read the *Boston Evening-Post*, *Boston Gazette*, *Boston Weekly News-Letter*, *Boston Weekly Post-Boy*, and *New England Weekly Journal*. New Yorkers enjoyed the *New-York Gazette, New-York Weekly Journal, New-York Weekly Post-Boy,* and *New-York Evening-Post*. The *American Weekly Mercury, Pennsylvania Gazette*, and *Pennsylvania Journal* were printed in Philadelphia. In the South, the *Maryland Gazette, Virginia Gazette*, and *South-Carolina Gazette* covered the news. Published weekly, the papers included news from Europe and the colonies as well as editorial comment via contributed letters. While some colonists subscribed to the papers, many more read the news in coffeehouses or neighbors' homes. By the 1730s, newspapers were becoming a vital part of the colonial information network.

Newspapers played a key role in spreading news of the religious events of the 1740s. Many papers significantly increased their coverage of religious news during the revival; for example, between 1735 and 1740, the *American Weekly Mercury, Pennsylvania Gazette, New-York*

Gazette, and *South-Carolina Gazette* enlarged their coverage of religion by 12.3 percent, 14.1 percent, 15.7 percent, and 14 percent, respectively. In Boston, between 1740 and 1745, the *Boston Evening-Post* and *Boston Gazette* each expanded their religious news coverage by approximately 15 percent.[13] Papers printed almost weekly reports on revivalist preaching, eye-witness accounts of revival meetings, and shocking stories of improper ordinations and church separations. No other colonial event of the 1740s, including the War of the Austrian Succession (1740-1748) and the Jacobite Rebellion (1745), came close to receiving as much coverage. Since colonial newspapers usually favored foreign news over domestic, the strong presence of local revival happenings during the 1740s is significant. At times, the papers were even unwitting conveyors of revival news as readers shared their copies. Scribbled by hand at the top of the *South-Carolina Gazette* for January 5, 1740, are the words, "The Revd Whitefield is to preach at French Church this morning," apparently a personal note to the next reader.[14]

The newspapers contained more than just factual reports on the religious events of the time, however. Consistent throughout the 1740s is extensive debate of the movement through letters contributed to the papers by both clergy and laymen, praising or denouncing virtually every aspect of the Awakening. Arguments over revivalists and their methods, lay preachers, church purity, antinomianism, and religious enthusiasm can be found in every newspaper during the 1740s, especially in the Boston papers, with some print wars lasting several months. In the colonies, as in England, Whitefield and his fellow revivalists learned that even negative press increased public interest. Many contributors saw in the religious events the hand of God, but just as many questioned the eventual outcome of the religious fervor.

The religious excitement brought an element of controversy to the papers that had not existed before to such a degree. One example from Boston illustrates this. On May 16, 1743, Thomas Fleet, printer of the *Boston Evening-Post* and in general an opponent of the revival, printed on the first page of his *Post* an extract from the "Declaration, Protestation, and Testimony of the suffering Remnant of the Anti-Popish, Anti-Lutheran, Anti-Prelarick, Anti-Whitefieldian, Anti-Erastian, Anti-Sectarian, true Presbyterian, Church of Christ in Scotland. Published against Mr. George Whitefield, and his Encouragers;

and against the Work at Cambuslang, and other Places." The declaration labeled revivalist George Whitefield an "Emissary of Satan" and the revival at Cambuslang, Scotland, a "mere Delusion of Satan."[15] In the *Post*, Fleet attributed the testimony against Whitefield and the Cambuslang revival to Ralph and Ebenezer Erskine and the Associate Presbytery, an extreme separatist and purist group of Calvinists in Scotland who had rejected Whitefield during his first tour of Scotland because Whitefield would not renounce his Anglican ordination vows and join the Associate Presbytery. Fleet taunted the Boston revivalist magazine *The Christian History* when he added his own note to the end of the declaration: "What will our Ch[risti]an Hi[sto]ry say to these Things?"

One week later on May 24, Thomas Prince, Jr., editor of the *Christian History*, used the *Boston Gazette* to criticize Fleet for not printing the authors' reasons for the declaration against Whitefield "that the World may see upon what a slighty Foundation so solemn a Testimony is rais'd." Prince also doubted that the Erskines, once correspondents and allies of Whitefield, had written the document and challenged Fleet to prove its authorship. Fleet's response one week later in the May 30 *Boston Evening-Post* contended that printers were not obliged to prove anything published in their newspapers: "There is not one Author in twenty can prove what he asserts, and how can you possibly expect a Printer should do it for him?"

The argument continued for several more weeks, with Fleet having the last word on July 4 and ending the squabble with an apology to his readers: "I now beg the Reader's Pardon for keeping him so long upon so trifling an Affair; and cannot but hope to be excused, as I have to do with one whose wrangling Conduct has again called me out to debate upon Points of no manner of Importance to the Publick." This dispute between two printers with opposing views of current religious happenings highlights the controversy and debate such "trifling" matters produced throughout the 1740s. Disagreement, personal attacks, and partisan politics became standard newspaper fare as printers reported on the religious events of the time.

Newspapers provide a unique window into the print history of the Awakening. First, because the material printed in newspapers was either reprinted from other papers or given to the printer by contributors, both advocates and detractors had a presence in the papers. The medium could not be claimed by either side as its own and was often used to defend and explain actions, attack opponents, offer questions, or rally support. Second, the sheer number of contributors to the papers ensured a variety of style, content, and opinion in each weekly issue. Laymen as well as clergymen contributed to the debate, and the occasional female voice was also heard. In addition, the medium was consistent and timely. Unlike pamphlets, journals, or published sermons, papers came out weekly and discussed events that had occurred only days before.

Scholars have identified the most general characteristics of newspaper reporting on the Awakening, particularly during its height. On the whole, reports on the revival were frequent and commonly appreciative during Whitefield's first preaching tour of the colonies, October 1739 through January 1741. The most contentious years of the revival occurred from 1741 through 1743, when Whitefield was absent from the colonies and both revivalists and their critics were attempting to define the movement and influence public opinion through the papers. By the end of 1743, reporting on the revival had greatly decreased, only to increase dramatically when Whitefield arrived for another tour of the colonies in October 1744. By the time Whitefield left for England in March 1748, interest in the movement had run its course.

However, no study has examined colonial newspaper reporting exhaustively and in enough detail to determine elements such as emergent trends in coverage as well as differences in regional reporting. This study provides a comprehensive, in-depth examination of the newspaper record of the religious events of the 1740s in an attempt to reveal information in three significant areas: changes over time in how the movement was presented by the majority of newspapers, specific differences in regional reporting, and significant shifts in the newspaper personalities of the main revivalists. This more complete and detailed reading of the newspaper coverage of the revival provides information not offered by earlier, more cursory studies.

To begin, the common colonial practice of reprinting items from other papers ensured that readers throughout the colonies heard the most important news of the revival, even if it happened far from home. Whitefield's preaching successes in the colony of South Carolina were reported eagerly by Boston papers and vice versa. Even local paper wars sometimes transcended regional boundaries when distant newspapers reprinted contributed letters from other papers. Local contributors could then comment on remote happenings, creating an intercolonial conversation. Only through the papers could readers in Boston, New York, Williamsburg, and Charleston debate issues as though they shared the same coffeehouse. Thus the prevalence of reprinted reports and contributed letters created a certain similarity of revival discussion and experience for readers. This experience shifted over time, however, as the papers emphasized different characteristics of the movement throughout the 1740s.

The papers also offered readers news and perspectives on the religious happenings that were decidedly local. Regional preaching stops by well-known revivalists were described in detail, while local contributors offered their opinions on the preacher and his message. Often, local "paper wars" would result as contributors battled each other in subsequent issues. Reporting in each region of the colonies had its own characteristics and central arguments.

Lastly, newspapers also consistently reported on the activities of the most popular revivalists, creating transcolonial "celebrities" in the process. The fact that Whitefield was known and welcomed in towns from New Hampshire to Georgia was due in large part to his presence in colonial newspapers. Three revivalists featured in the papers reached this "celebrity" status—Whitefield, Gilbert Tennent, and James Davenport—and each of these revivalists enjoyed his own persona, his own public image, in the newspapers. Yet, this image also shifted over time, sometimes to the revivalist's detriment.

To examine in detail the shifts and characteristics of colonial reporting on the Awakening, one must begin by selecting starting and ending dates. The dates 1739-1745 are usually considered the key years of the movement as they coincide with the first and part of the second of George Whitefield's colonial preaching tours; however, a case can be made for examining the papers through 1748, which is the year Whitefield ended his second preaching tour of the colonies. During the years 1739-1748, inclusive, an examination of all English-language colonial newspapers found 1598 newspaper items, including reprints, which related to revival events. The printed items were almost evenly split between news and opinion, with 52 percent of the items being news reports and the rest contributed letters or excerpts from other published writings.[16]

This examination of how colonial newspapers portrayed the religious events of the 1740s is organized into three chapters. Chapter 1 examines the key characteristics of the Awakening presented by the colonial newspapers and how reporting on the movement changed during the 1740s. Chapter 2 identifies how reporting varied by region, examining the characteristics and paper wars of the different regions of the colonies. George Whitefield, Gilbert Tennent, and James Davenport were the only revivalists who appeared with any regularity in the newspapers, so chapter 3 examines how these men appeared in the papers and how their personas shifted over time. Appendix 1 offers methodological considerations while appendix 2 presents a table showing the number of positive, negative, and neutral items on the revival printed by each newspaper for the years 1739 through 1748, inclusive. Shifting presentations of the revival, regional differences, and changes in reporting on the major personalities of the revival all make the newspaper record of the Awakening an intriguing and informative window into the major colonial event of the 1740s.

NOTES

1. Reprinted from the English periodical *Common Sense* for April 28, 1739.

2. See the *New-York Gazette*, November 26, 1739, for the first newspaper article on the controversy.

3. David A. Copeland, *Colonial American Newspapers: Character and Content* (Newark: University of Delaware Press, 1997), 218. According to James N. Green, "From 1740 to 1743, the annual value of imports from London to Pennsylvania had soared from two to three times its previous annual average" (James N. Green, "Part I. English Books and Printing in the Age of Franklin," in *The Colonial Book in the Atlantic World*, eds. Hugh Amory and David D. Hall, vol. 1, *A History of the Book in America*, 248-98 (Cambridge, MA: Cambridge University Press, 2000), 263.

4. Frank Lambert, *Inventing the "Great Awakening"* (Princeton, NJ: Princeton University Press, 1999), 252, 213.

5. David D. Hall, "Part I. The Atlantic Economy in the Eighteenth Century," in *The Colonial Book in the Atlantic World*, eds. Hugh Amory and

David D. Hall, vol. 1, *A History of the Book in America*, 152-62 (Cambridge, MA: Cambridge University Press, 2000), 156.

6. Charles E. Hambrick-Stowe, "The Spirit of the Old Writers: Print Media, the Great Awakening, and Continuity in New England," in *Communication and Change in American Religious History* ed. Leonard I. Sweet, 128-35 (Grand Rapids, MI: Eerdmans, 1993), 130.

7. Jon Butler, "Enthusiasm Described and Decried: The Great Awakening as Interpretive Fiction," *The Journal of American History*, 69 (1982): 305-25.

8. Joseph A. Conforti, *Jonathan Edwards, Religious Tradition and American Culture* (Chapel Hill: University of North Carolina Press, 1995), 12-13.

9. Lambert, *Inventing*, 10.

10. Green, "English Books and Printing," 260.

11. Alan Heimert and Perry Miller, eds., *The Great Awakening: Documents Illustrating the Crisis and Its Consequences*, American Heritage Series 34 (New York: Bobbs-Merrill, 1967), 255.

12. Charles E. Clark, *The Public Prints: The Newspaper in Anglo-American Culture, 1665-1740* (New York: Oxford University Press, 1994), 257.

13. These numbers are taken from Copeland, *Colonial American Newspapers*, 291-93.

14. The church mentioned is probably the French Protestant Church of Charleston, founded by Huguenots in approximately 1681.

15. Under the pastoral leadership of the Rev. William Macculloch, the village of Cambuslang began experiencing revival in the spring of 1742. Whitefield traveled to Cambuslang in June 1742 to participate in the excitement, raising the ire of those who opposed him in Scotland.

16. For specific findings, please see Lisa Herb Smith, "The First Great Awakening in American Newspapers, 1739-48," (PhD diss., University of Delaware, 1998).

CHAPTER 1

Reporting the Awakening

I saw before me a Cloud or fog, rising—I first thought—off from the great river. But as I came nearer the road I heard a noise, something like a low rumbling thunder, and I presently found it was the rumbling of horses feet coming down the road and this Cloud was a Cloud of dust made by the running of horses feet. . . . Every hors seemed to go with all his might to carry his rider to hear the news from heaven for the saving of their Souls.

Nathan Cole, 1740[1]

On December 19, 1739, a weary and feverish George Whitefield arrived at an inn in North Carolina, having traveled twenty-six miles on horseback that day. The English itinerant preacher had landed in America less than two months earlier and had spent those weeks preaching to record crowds throughout the Middle Colonies on the first leg of an intercolonial preaching tour. Upon learning the identity of their exhausted guest, the innkeeper and his wife could not contain their pleasure at housing the most famous man in the colonies. Even the host's son-in-law, who lived about three miles away, had read of Whitefield in the newspapers and hoped someday to hear the evangelist preach.[2]

While this account of Whitefield's fame comes from the man himself, other contemporary documents support the fact that Whitefield and the movement he represented were well-known enough throughout the colonies that an innkeeper and his family in rural North Carolina knew of Whitefield's ministry and had followed his travels. For the colonies, the Awakening was the first "national event," to use the words of Whitefield biographer Frank Lambert.[3] Contemporary writings by figures as diverse as Virginia Governor William Gooch, Maryland physician Alexander Hamilton, and Anglican Commissary Alexander Garden in South Carolina all mention the revival and reveal that most colonists were aware of the movement as well as its key supporters and opponents. Although modern scholars have debated the role revivalists played in "creating" a revival out of the scattered religious events of the early 1740s, there is little argument that revival supporters and detractors alike admitted that religion was the topic of the day.

Richard Brown notes that virtually all New England farmers, regardless of location, were affected by the movement and aware of the leading revivalists.[4] The experience of Connecticut farmer Isaac Backus (1724-1806) shows the extent of the movement. During the summer of 1741, Backus heard several of the most prominent itinerant preachers of the revival such as Benjamin Pomeroy, Eleazer Wheelock, Jedidiah Mills, and James Davenport as they passed through his small town of Norwich. Backus notes their effect on the town:

> Although I was often warned and Exorted [sic] (especially by my godly mother), To fly from the Wrath to come—yet I Never was under any Powerful Conviction Till the year 1741. When it pleased the Lord to cause a very general awakening Thro' the Land; especially in Norwich The work was so remarkable that the children & yong [sic] People were broke off from Their Plays & frolics. . . . Many were Hopefully Converted & many others under Powerful Conviction & a general thoughtfulness seemed to appear on the minds of people.[5]

Backus was later converted and became ordained as a Baptist minister. Colonists in the Middle Colonies and the South could share similar experiences with traveling revivalists and conversion.

Colonial newspapers played a key role in disseminating news of the revival. During Whitefield's first two preaching tours of the colonies and the years in between (1739-1748), colonial newspapers printed 1598 newspaper notices related to the Awakening. No other contemporaneous event comes close to receiving that amount of coverage. In the ten-year period of newspaper reporting on the revival, negative coverage slightly outnumbered positive, 554 items to 438, while neutral coverage was the most frequent at 606.[6] Letters and news reports were almost equal in number, with 761 letters and 837 news reports appearing during the period.

American newspapers were only a half-century old when Whitefield landed on American shores. The first colonial newspaper, Boston's *Publick Occurrences Both Forreign and Domestic*, began its run on September 25, 1690, but lasted only one issue, and the next American newspaper did not appear until fourteen years later. By the early 1740s, eleven English-language newspapers were publishing—five in Boston, two in New York, two in Philadelphia, one in Virginia, and one in South Carolina.[7]

The men who printed the newspapers for colonial America were printers by trade who, when one of them began a weekly paper, functioned as the copy editor, compositor, reporter, pressman, and editorialist.[8] Printing a newspaper was risky business as a weekly paper required substantial human and material resources. Charles E. Clark has estimated that 600 copies of a four-page newspaper would have required twenty-eight hours of work from a good compositor, at least five hours of press time, and one and a quarter reams of paper.[9] Theoretically, 600 copies would cost a printer about thirty shillings. To offset these expenses, the printer relied on subscriptions and advertisements. Advertising fees were usually paid in cash when the advertisement was placed, but yearly subscriptions, a more important source of income, were difficult to collect. Subscribers were often in arrears, sometimes for years. Newspaper publishing could be a lucrative aspect of a printing business, supplementing competitive job printing, but it could also be disastrous—of the sixty newspapers begun in the colonies before 1760, ten failed before a year had passed and another ten closed after less than four years.[10]

By the time the religious excitement of the 1740s began, colonial newspapers were fairly standardized. Printed on folio half-sheets and appearing weekly, the papers primarily offered readers news of European events that had occurred from six weeks to six months previously. Local news followed news from the Continent, and creativity was at a minimum.[11] Sensational stories of tragedies, acts of divine providence, public executions, and scientific discoveries also were eagerly noted by the papers, although investigative reporting to unearth such stories was nonexistent. Printers received their news from English newspapers and papers from other colonies, ship captains and other visitors as they arrived in town, government officials, and correspondents from abroad. Contributed letters were also printed in the papers, offering reader opinions on current topics. Subscribers could be found in locations far from the publishing cities as the postal service carried newspapers to the outlying areas. Clark has estimated that one newspaper was printed for every 125 colonists by 1740.[12]

When one examines the newspaper record of the religious events of the 1740s, one dominant story emerges across colonies and newspapers. Several factors can account for the existence of this dominant story. Whitefield's presence at the center of the movement certainly caused a similarity of experience in all parts of the colonies. Listeners' responses to Whitefield and other revivalists were often ritualistic in nature, as noted by historians such as Marilyn J. Westerkamp: "All observers and historians agree that revival participants everywhere swooned, shouted, panted, and convulsed. They indulged in ritualized spontaneity, traditional creativity, structured outbursts; they behaved in patterns so easily recognized and compared that contemporary observers and scholars alike have since proclaimed 'A Great Awakening.'"[13] Contemporaneous newspaper descriptions of conversions contain common elements and utilize similar language. The converted struggle for a time under conviction of sin, experience a defined moment when God's truth illuminates the soul, and enjoy subsequent raptures of joy. Typical is a report in the May 13, 1742, *Pennsylvania Gazette* describing conversions in Scotland: "[T]hey are commonly three Days under terrible Convictions, and faint away; then they are carried to the Ministers House, from which they return in the greatest Raptures of Joy and Comfort."

The itinerant preaching style of Whitefield and other revivalists also raised common intellectual concerns throughout the colonies, such as the implications of the movement for colonial theology and religious practice. Key issues such as the emotionalism and enthusiasm of the revival, lay and itinerant preaching, church splits and unorthodox ordinations, and the divisiveness of some revivalists were discussed from the pulpit, in the newspapers, at the coffeehouses, and through pamphlets and treatises.

As many modern scholars have noted, revivalists and their opponents made concerted efforts to present one, consistent story of the revival to readers, using writings such as pamphlets, printed sermons, newspaper reports and letters, and published journals to "invent" competing versions of the movement to suit their own ends.[14] While supporters presented a revival that was sweeping and powerful, detractors used the same media to offer their own counter-invention of events as religious zeal gone to harmful extremes.

Perhaps the primary reason for the uniformity of newspaper reporting on the revival was the eighteenth-century practice of reprinting stories from other newspapers regularly and without editing. Readers could easily follow the progress of Whitefield and other revivalists throughout the colonies through reprinted notices in their local papers. For example, the *Pennsylvania Gazette*'s notice on November 8, 1739, that Whitefield had arrived in Philadelphia to begin his preaching tour was reprinted less than a week later by three Boston papers.[15] On November 29, both Philadelphia papers, Andrew Bradford's *American Weekly Mercury* and Benjamin Franklin's *Pennsylvania Gazette*, printed the same report on the evangelist's preaching activities in and around Philadelphia. The story was reprinted verbatim by the *Boston Weekly Post-Boy* (December 10), *Boston Evening-Post* (December 12), *Boston Weekly News-Letter* (December 13), and *New England Weekly Journal* (December 11) in Boston; the *New-York Gazette* (December 10); and the *Virginia Gazette* (January 18, 1740). Whitefield's arrival in Savannah, Georgia, on January 10, 1740, was noted by the *South-Carolina Gazette* on February 2, and papers in Philadelphia, New York, and Boston reprinted the article.[16] Even letters contributed to one paper were reprinted by other papers if the letter was interesting, sensational, or concerned a well-known revivalist such as Whitefield.

Fully 30 percent, or 476 items, of the 1598 revival-related notices printed in the papers from 1739 through 1748 were reprints.[17] More reprints appeared in the early and later years of the revival when decreased controversy led to less original reporting and commentary. For example, during 1739, 55 percent of all American newspaper articles on the revival were reprints, and Whitefield figured in all but four reprinted items. During the key years of controversy in the colonies, 1741-1745, reprints accounted for an average of only approximately 23 percent of total newspaper notices. Most reprints were factual reports on the travels of key revivalists, with Whitefield appearing the most often. These reprintings ensured that readers everywhere received similar news of the revival and were kept informed of developments, regardless of location.

Newspapers printed both news reports and contributed commentary on the revival. In general, news reports in all papers were inserted by the printer and included details such as the preacher and location of the sermon, the number of listeners, the amount of money collected, and the general response of the audience to the speaker. The majority of the reports were neutral in tone; of the 837 news reports in colonial papers from 1739 through 1748, almost 60 percent were impartial. Figure 1.1 reveals the number and tone of news reports printed during the years 1739-1748 (see figures at the end of this chapter). Since colonial newspapers did not employ reporters in the modern sense, the printer received his news from eye-witnesses, other newspapers, and letters. Besides news of the movement, commentary on the revival came in the form of letters to the printer, usually from local clergymen and laymen. Unlike news reports, contributed letters were seldom impartial; of the 761 letters printed in the papers during the same years, less than 20 percent were neutral. Figure 1.2 shows the number and tone of the printed letters.[18] Although each paper carried unique letters, the major topics of the revival such as emotionalism, lay preaching, and the censorious nature of the revival were frequently discussed in all the papers.

On another level, however, although one dominant story does emerge from the papers, this story does not remain static throughout the life span of the revival. The tone and frequency of newspaper reporting on the movement changed significantly over the ten years that spanned Whitefield's first and second preaching tours of the colonies, as Figure 1.3 reveals. Issues that were hardly present in the papers during Whitefield's first tour dominated the papers during his second tour. American revivalists who were briefly mentioned in the papers while Whitefield was in the colonies rose to prominence during his absence. Even the revival itself appeared differently in the papers at the beginning of the 1740s than it did during the mid-1740s.

A discussion of one representative colonial newspaper during the years spanning Whitefield's first two colonial preaching tours, 1739-1748, illustrates the general trends in reporting on the Awakening. Benjamin Franklin, printer of the *Pennsylvania Gazette*, enjoyed a friendship with Whitefield, often hosting Whitefield when he visited Philadelphia. Franklin was also Whitefield's primary colonial printer, publishing his journals and letters as well as many reports in the *Gazette* on the evangelist. Franklin did not, however, share Whitefield's evangelical beliefs.

Franklin printed more items on the revival in his *Gazette* than did any other newspaper outside of Boston. The *Gazette*'s total of 164 items printed during the years 1739-1748 is exceeded only by the *Boston Evening-Post* with 345 and the *Boston Gazette* with 203. Franklin's coverage of the revival tended toward the positive, but was overall even-handed—the *Gazette* printed a total of fifty-nine positive items, twenty-six negative items, and seventy-nine neutral items. One hundred twelve news reports appeared in the *Gazette*, while fifty-two letters were printed. Overall, the *Gazette*'s reporting on the religious events of the 1740s reflects the general trends seen in papers throughout the colonies.

EARLY REPORTING ON THE AWAKENING

Reporting on the Awakening throughout the colonies during the first two years focused heavily on Whitefield, and he represented the movement for most American colonists. When the evangelist arrived in what is now Lewes, Delaware, for his first colonial preaching tour in October 1739, the papers had reprinted more than eighty items regarding Whitefield and the revival in England in the ten months leading up to his arrival. Like many other newspaper printers, Franklin had offered reprints on Whitefield's preaching from London papers; a total of three appeared in the *Gazette* before Whitefield landed. Once Whitefield arrived in the colonies in October 1739, Franklin began covering the evangelist more regularly, reprinting reports from papers in Boston and New York. This same approach was followed by most other newspaper printers throughout the colonies.

What is noteworthy about Whitefield's entrance into the American newspaper scene is its explosiveness. Approximately seventy-five newspaper items related to Whitefield appeared in the colonial papers during the first two months of Whitefield's visit, almost the same number that had appeared during the preceding ten months. Franklin printed nine items in the first two months after Whitefield's arrival—four letters and five news reports.

Newspaper reporting on the movement was also overwhelmingly positive during the early years of the 1740s. Letters printed in the papers supporting the movement outnumbered those against it by a margin of almost three to one. In 1740 alone, Franklin printed forty-four items on the revival in the *Gazette*, only three of which were critical of the movement. An example of Franklin's reporting appeared on May 22, 1740, in both the *Pennsylvania Gazette* and Franklin's competitor in the city, the *American Weekly Mercury*:

> This Evening the Reverend Mr. Whitefield went on board his Sloop here, in order to sail for Georgia. On Sunday he preached twice at Philadelphia, and in the Evening (when he preached his Farewell Sermon) it is supposed he had near 20000 hearers. . . . The Presence of God was much seen in the Assemblies, especially at Nottingham and Fogs [Faggs] Mannor, where the People were under such deep Soul Distress, that by their Cries they almost drown'd his Voice.

The same report was reprinted in the *New England Weekly Journal* (June 3) and the *Boston Weekly News-Letter* (June 5).

In addition to emphasizing Whitefield and being generally positive toward the revival, newspaper reporting on the movement during the early years also emphasized the extensiveness of the Awakening. Even an occasional reader of American papers during this time would have been convinced that the colonies were experiencing a general revitalization of religion. Although some disputed the value and propriety of the revival, all agreed that religion was the topic of the day. During Whitefield's first tour, 366 items appeared in the newspapers regarding the revival. Franklin's *Gazette* offered thirty-nine items.

Newspaper coverage of the most famous revivalist preachers of the Awakening was frequent and detailed. Of course Whitefield's travels were reported, but lesser known revivalists also received steady coverage in the papers. Presbyterian minister Gilbert Tennent's arrival in New England in December 1740 for a preaching tour was noted immediately by the *New England Weekly Journal*:

On Saturday last came hither, by Land from New Brunswick in the Jerseys, the Rev. Mr. Gilbert Tennent, who preach'd twice the next Day at the Rev. Mr. Webb's Meeting House, and yesterday in the afternoon he preach'd a Lecture at the same Place, to very great Acceptance. He is to preach this Evening's Lecture at Dr. Colman's Meeting House in Brattle-Street. Tomorrow about three o'Clock afternoon he will preach a Lecture at the Old South Meeting House; and on Thursday next he is to preach the Lecture at the usual Time and Place. (December 16, 1740)

Tennent was accorded the same courtesy that Whitefield received— papers published his upcoming lecture sites so interested readers could attend. The papers published seventeen items related to Tennent's 1740/1741 New England preaching tour alone, only two of which were negative.[19] As late as April 15, 1742, a letter from Tennent appeared in the *Boston Weekly News-Letter* regarding his 1740-1741 New England tour.

Franklin's experience covering Tennent's New England preaching tour reveals the impact the revival had on newspaper printing. During Tennent's tour, Franklin reprinted two news reports from Boston papers detailing Tennent's travels.[20] When Tennent contributed a letter to the *Boston Weekly News-Letter* on July 22, 1742, questioning some of his own itinerant practices, Franklin reprinted it in his *Gazette* on August 12. Local contributors quickly responded to Tennent's reprinted letter, causing Franklin to print five more letters on Tennent, with one from Tennent himself.[21]

The papers also noted the increased publication of religious writing during the revival, devoting space to advertisements and commentary on recently published works and fueling a belief in the revival's pervasiveness. On March 15, 1740, the *South-Carolina Gazette* reported that in Philadelphia and New York: "Sermons, which used to be the greatest Drug, are now the only Books in Demand." Some works received special attention in the papers. The *Boston Evening-Post* printed letters from extreme revivalists against moderate revivalist Jonathan Dickinson's *A Display of God's Special Grace* (December 6, 1742). Franklin printed Whitefield's *Three Letters From the Reverend Mr. G. Whitefield: Viz. Letter I. To a Friend in London, concerning Archbishop Tillotson. Letter II. To the same on the same Subject. Letter III. To the Inhabitants of Maryland, Virginia, North and South-Carolina, concerning their Negroes* (Philadelphia, 1740) in 1740, but also printed the letters in his *Pennsylvania Gazette* on April 10 and April 17, 1740.

Franklin's coverage of the movement reveals another characteristic seen in reporting on the Awakening during its early years—many of the newspaper reports emphasized the power of the revival experience. This power tended to be revealed in two ways in the reporting: by the effects on the local region/city and by the physical responses of the listeners. The most frequent effect of revivalist preaching noted by the papers is the continuance of an interest in religion after the visiting preacher had left the city. For example, news items such as the following printed in the *South-Carolina Gazette* on March 15, 1740, appeared frequently in the early years: "We hear from Philadelphia and New York, that since Mr. Whitefield's preaching in those Places, several Week-Day Lectures have been set up, which are much crowded." Reports of revival activity from local clergymen also appeared in the papers, such as this example from the Rev. John Owen of Groton, Connecticut: "As to the State of Religion here, it appears flourishing and I hope increasing. It is indeed an extraordinary time. . . . There has been about an Hundred of my Congregation hopefully Converted and brought to the saving Knowledge of Christ in about 5 or 6 months past; and great Numbers are still under awakening Convictions."[22] On June 12, 1740, Franklin noted in his *Pennsylvania Gazette* the effect Whitefield's preaching had on Philadelphia:

> The Alteration in the Face of Religion here is altogether surprizing. Never did People show so great a Willingness to attend Sermons, nor the Preachers greater Zeal and Diligence in performing the Duties of their Function. Religion is become the Subject of most Conversations. No Books are in Request but those of Piety and Devotion; and instead of idle Songs and Ballads, the People are every where entertaining themselves with Psalms, Hymns and Spiritual Songs. All which, under God, is owing to the successful Labours of the Rev. Mr. Whitefield.

Franklin's report was reprinted by all four Boston papers and by the *South-Carolina Gazette.*[23] Although covered in detail in chapter 3, it is noteworthy here that when Franklin printed a report on May 1, 1740, that the dancing school had closed down since Whitefield's preaching, the report of the school's closing was reprinted by the *Boston Evening-*

Post on May 12 and the *New England Weekly Journal* on May 13, while the rebuttal which appeared in the next issue of the *Pennsylvania Gazette* was not.

The physical responses of revival participants were often reported by the papers in the early years and presented a movement that appeared to be indeed strangely powerful. An item in the *South-Carolina Gazette* for March 22, 1740, printed soon after Whitefield preached in that colony, is representative: "Every time he preach'd, there was a solemn Silence and Seriousness upon the Face of his crowded Audience." The *American Weekly Mercury* reprinted the *South-Carolina Gazette* story for its Philadelphia readers on May 29. While the awestruck silence of listeners was often noted by the papers in the early years, the more dramatic responses such as fainting, crying out, or shaking were reported in the papers as well. Two letters from New England printed in the June 21, 1742, *South-Carolina Gazette* mentioned that followers of the "new Way" exhibited strange behaviors such as barking like dogs and "Foaming or Fainting." Often, strong emotional responses were reported as listeners experienced terror and distress from conviction of sin until being assured that they had received God's forgiveness and salvation. On July 16, 1741, the *American Weekly Mercury* printed a letter from a layman in New Light clergyman George Griswold's parish in East Lyme, Connecticut. The writer described the effects itinerant preacher Jonathan Parsons produced at a recent service: "[S]uch a Power of the Divine Spirit accompanying the preached Gospel I had then never seen, about 40 Persons were then deeply Wounded, almost 20 of them in such anguish of Soul as I never beheld before, 7 died away with Fear & Horror." A similar response occurred in Parsons' own parish according to the writer: "[T]he Worship was interrupted, near 100 Persons in deep anguish and about 60 crying out aloud, about 30 died away with their great Horror, and some were with Difficulty brought to again." Yet many also exhibited "good Evidence of the New Birth, some rejoicing with Joy unspeakable, my own Children are Sharers in the Work."

What was not emphasized by the newspapers in the early years of reporting on the Awakening is as interesting as what was emphasized. Absent from the papers are personal testimonies of spiritual awakening, except in the occasional report from a pastor regarding the effects of the revival on his congregation. Except for the Rev. Jonathan Arnold of New York, personal interactions with the best-known revivalists were not reported and papers rarely reported which biblical passages revivalists preached on or details of the sermons. In general, newspaper reporting in the early years of the 1740s emphasized the explosiveness of Whitefield's entry into the colonies, and presented the movement he represented as powerful, extensive, and generally positive.

REPORTING AFTER WHITEFIELD'S FIRST PREACHING TOUR

Whitefield left the colonies in January 1741, and the effect on news reporting on the Awakening was immediate. Coverage was initially less frequent and less supportive of the revival. The eleven months following Whitefield's departure saw much less reporting on the movement with only 138 items. Franklin printed less than half the number of revival-related items in 1741 than he had in 1740. And, for the first time, the number of negative items essentially equaled the number of positive items, although there were still many neutral items printed. News items continued to outpace contributed letters, seventy-three to sixty-five, but the margin of difference was much less.

One year later in 1742, reporting on the revival increased again, almost reaching the totals during Whitefield's 1739-1741 preaching tour, yet this time, the coverage was significantly different. The strongest influence on reporting on the revival after 1741 was the increasingly negative attitude toward the movement that began after Whitefield left the colonies. Whitefield's criticisms of established church traditions and "dead" religious practice created a backlash against the evangelist and his American counterparts. The high rate of church disagreements and splits as well as the increase in the controversial practice of itinerant preaching turned many against the movement. The Rev. James Davenport's itinerant travels in the spring and summer of 1742, reportedly characterized by bizarre and censorious behavior, also contributed to concern. When Whitefield returned to the colonies for a second preaching tour in October 1744, his arrival only added to the controversy.

Like most printers, Franklin increased his coverage of the Awakening in 1742, printing twenty-two items on the movement, almost double the thirteen items he had printed in 1741. Franklin also followed many of the key controversies for his *Gazette* readers. Revivalist Gilbert Tennent's letter repenting of his early zeal was featured in the Boston papers and reprinted by Franklin on August 12, 1742. Reports on James Davenport's deportation from both Connecticut and Massachusetts were reprinted by Franklin from the Boston papers. In 1743, twenty items appeared in the *Gazette* on the revival.

The increasingly negative attitude toward the movement had two immediate effects on newspaper coverage of the Awakening after 1741. First, negative items on the Awakening outnumbered positive items in 1742 for the first time by a shocking margin—146 negative items to 36 positive items, with 46 neutral items.[24] This trend continued through 1745. Second, letters outnumbered news reports for the first time as readers debated the issues raised by the revival. One hundred forty-five letters were printed as compared to only eighty-three news items, despite the fact that American revivalists such as James Davenport continued to receive coverage of their itinerant preaching tours. Letters continued to outnumber news reports through 1745, as shown in Figure 1.4.

One story reported by Franklin in the summer of 1741 reveals the new direction reporting on the revival would soon go. The Philadelphia Synod of the Presbyterian denomination held its annual meeting in Philadelphia beginning on May 27, 1741, and disagreements over the Awakening quickly took center stage. The synod had been plagued for years by arguments over itinerant preaching, ministerial candidate ordination, and forced subscription to the Westminster Confession of Faith. In 1740, the pro-revival New Brunswick Presbytery objected to recent laws by the synod in their *Apology of the Presbytery of New-Brunswick* (Philadelphia, 1741). When the 1741 synod began, Robert Cross of the Philadelphia Presbytery presented to the synod a written protestation signed by twelve anti-revival pastors and ten elders, which was designed to force the revivalists from the synod if they did not conform. Finding themselves in the minority, although Gilbert Tennent later declared the vote was split evenly, the revivalists withdrew and promptly formed their own synod with the New Brunswick and Londonderry Presbyteries.[25]

The event was reported by Benjamin Franklin in the *Pennsylvania Gazette* on June 11, 1741:

> On the 25th of the last Month, the Presbyterian Synod opened their Session in this City; and after several Days spent in Debates on the Rights of the Presbyteries, &c., a Protestation was entred into, on the first Instant, and signed by 12 Ministers and 8 Members then present, by which the Rev. Messirs. the Tennents, and their Adherents, are excluded the Synod, and declared to have forfeited their Right of sitting and voting as Members thereof. The excluded Brethren immediately withdrew, and met by themselves in another Place. 'Tis said that the Number of the Excluded was nearly equal to that of the Synod remaining. The Protestation, containing the Reasons of their Conduct, is now publish'd by Order of the Synod.

Franklin's calm, objective tone belied the acrimony and import of the situation. The story was quickly reprinted by the *Boston Gazette* (June 22), *Boston Weekly Post-Boy* (June 22), *New England Weekly Journal* (June 23), and *South-Carolina Gazette* (July 23). Old Side Presbyterians Robert Cross and John Thomson both published pamphlets defending the actions of the synod, while New Side revivalists Samuel Blair and Gilbert Tennent defended the revivalists.[26] Interest in the controversy was so strong in Boston that three weeks later on July 6, the *Boston Weekly Post-Boy* published an excerpt from Cross' original protestation.[27] Even one year later, Franklin printed "A Protestation Presented to the Synod of Philadelphia," signed by ten clergymen protesting the exclusion of the members of the New Brunswick Presbytery from the Philadelphia Synod because the exclusion was done as an "illegal and unprecedented Procedure, contrary to the Rules of the Gospel, and subversive of our excellent Constitution." The protestation declared the excluded brethren members of the Synod, proclaimed the Awakening a "Work of Divine Power and Grace," and condemned "all divisive and irregular Methods and Practices by which the Peace and good Order of our Churches have been broken in upon."

Franklin's coverage of the Presbyterian Synod split reveals the new direction reporting on the Awakening would take after 1741. More reports would focus on church splits and revival opposition, more letters would be printed by the papers questioning revival practices and theology, and negative reporting would increase significantly. In his *Pennsylvania Gazette*, Franklin printed more negative items than positive for the years 1742, 1743, and 1744, although neutral items outnumbered negative in 1743 and 1744. He also printed more letters than news reports in 1742 and 1743.

NEW DIRECTIONS IN REPORTING

Not surprisingly, the increased controversy surrounding the Awakening and the turn toward more negative reporting and more debate changed how the revival appeared in the newspapers. While the power, range, and positive effects of the movement had been emphasized during Whitefield's 1739-1741 visit, both the nature of the Awakening and its effects appeared very differently after 1741. Specifically, many reports after 1741 presented the nature of the Awakening as controversial, irrational, and dangerous.

The controversy caused by Whitefield and other revivalists appeared often in the papers after 1741. American revivalists such as Gilbert Tennent, James Davenport, Andrew Croswell, John Moorhead, Samuel Buell, Benjamin Pomeroy, and Nathaniel and Daniel Rogers all received negative coverage in the papers after 1741. For example, an anonymous contributor to the January 12, 1741, *Boston Weekly Post-Boy* criticized Tennent's decision to leave his congregation for several months to conduct a New England preaching tour. Criticism of Davenport was common, particularly during his ill-fated preaching tours through Connecticut and Massachusetts in the spring and summer of 1742. When both colonies declared Davenport *non compos mentis*, the papers eagerly followed the events.[28] The increase in contributed letters printed in the papers assured readers more controversy as writers battled over the practices and effects associated with the Awakening.

Fights within the revival camp particularly were newsworthy, such as Whitefield's disagreement with John Wesley over predestination or extreme revivalist Andrew Croswell's attack on moderate Jonathan Dickinson in the *Boston Evening-Post* on December 6, 1742. Church separations were also reported by the papers, especially when the separation involved an itinerant preacher. When revival opponent Rev.

Samuel Mather and his supporters left the Second Church of Christ in Boston to form their own fellowship, both the *Boston Evening-Post* and the *Boston Weekly Post-Boy* for February 1, 1742, printed lengthy reports. Both papers followed the story a few months later when the new fellowship erected a permanent church building.[29]

Franklin included more controversy in his *Gazette* after 1741 as well. For example, on July 22, 1742, a letter by Gilbert Tennent was printed in the *Boston Weekly News-Letter* which condemned and questioned many revival practices as well as some actions of James Davenport. Franklin reprinted the letter in his *Gazette* on August 12, 1742. Five subsequent letters appeared in the *Gazette* debating the issues raised by Tennent's letter, including an additional letter from Tennent himself.[30] Five reprints appeared as well in papers in both New England and the South.[31]

Besides being controversial, the revival was also portrayed in the papers after 1741 as tending toward irrationality. A *Boston Evening-Post* reader offered his view of revivalists on January 4, 1742: "Some Preachers of late having declared themselves mortal Foes to Humane Reason, in Matters of Religion, as a Thing dangerous and destructive to the Souls of Men, and are so frequently heard snarling at REASON (that fair Offspring of the Father of Lights) in a most rude and opprobrious Manner, that one may well INFER, they have little or no Part or Lot in that Matter." Another *Post* contributor on August 23, 1742, worried that the "Fancies of a Man's own Brain" would substitute for "Reason and Revelation." "A modest Proposal for the Destruction of Reason" appeared in the *Boston Evening-Post* on June 7, 1742, and satirized the New Light Shepherd's Tent seminary by suggesting that plaster be applied to the heads of seminarians directly over the place where Reason resides in the brain.[32] The Boston papers printed numerous letters attacking the revivalist magazine *The Christian History*, one of which claimed the serial discredited the "Use of Reason, Learning and Study, in Preaching." The same letter also criticized the "unpremeditated, unconnected immethodical Harrangues [sic] so much in Vogue among the New Lights."[33]

The papers also printed stories of extreme religious fervor, often termed "enthusiasm," which emphasized the irrationality of the movement.[34] Franklin, for example, reprinted a report from England in his

Pennsylvania Gazette on October 28, 1742, of a man making himself a eunuch "for the Kingdom of Heaven's Sake." The story was reprinted by the *Boston Evening-Post* (November 8), *Boston Weekly Post-Boy* (November 8), *Boston Weekly News-Letter* (November 12), and *South-Carolina Gazette* (December 3). Revivalists were also compared to other religious extremists from history; the *Boston Evening-Post* for March 22, 1742, printed South Carolina Commissary Alexander Garden's comparison of revivalists to the Dutartes, a sect in South Carolina that committed atrocious acts in the name of religion.[35] The story was reprinted by the *New-York Weekly Journal* on April 12. On July 19, 1742, during James Davenport's Boston preaching tour, the *Post* printed "The Story of William Hacket the Enthusiast," an Elizabethan zealot who declared himself king of the world and was subsequently executed. The story was reprinted by the *New-York Weekly Journal* on August 16. The revival was even compared to the Salem witchcraft trials in the *Boston Weekly News-Letter* of December 8, 1743.

The revival also began to be portrayed in the papers as dangerous. For example, printers included many accounts of revivalism gone awry. On April 12, 1742, the *Boston Weekly Post-Boy* carried the story of a young man who frequented New Light meetings and ultimately drowned himself. The *American Weekly Mercury* (April 22), *New-York Weekly Journal* (May 3), and *South-Carolina Gazette* (June 21) reprinted the account. On July 19, 1742, the *Boston Weekly Post-Boy* reported that a woman in South Carolina, "a great favourer of the New-light Men," hanged herself "upon Account of Religion." The *American Weekly Mercury* reprinted the report for Philadelphians on July 29. Both the *Mercury* (August 5) and the *Boston Weekly Post-Boy* (August 9) reprinted a report from the August 2, 1742, issue of the *New-York Weekly Journal* of a man under "Convictions" hanging himself "with his Knees not above 3 Inches from the Ground." On October 6, 1746, the *Boston Evening-Post* reported that a Manchester, England, man had murdered his apprentice in "a Fit of Enthusiastick Frenzy," while the *Maryland Gazette* recorded a murder that occurred between two men "debating about Religion" (September 15, 1747).

Colonial newspapers reprinted stories from England on riots and fights prompted by the revival, detailing the resulting injuries and damages.[36] On July 19, 1745, the *Boston Weekly News-Letter* reported from

Exeter, England, that Methodists in England entering their place of worship had been attacked by a mob who "pelted them as they went in and daub'd them with Dung, Potatoes, Mud, &c. and before they came out were encreas'd to some Thousands, together with the Spectators, who, as the People came out, threw them in the Dirt, trampled on them, and beat all without Exception." The *Maryland Gazette* reprinted the story on August 16. The most significant American tragedy associated with revival crowds occurred in southern Boston on September 22, 1740, before Whitefield was to preach at the Rev. Samuel Checkley's meetinghouse. A mass panic began when someone shouted that the upper galleries were giving way, and five people were killed. Papers in New York and Philadelphia reported the event, and four of the five Boston papers carried the story, each presenting its own original report.[37]

Reader interest in strange and sensational events was no different in the eighteenth century than it is today. Reports of thunderstorms, comets, fires, and plagues were common in colonial papers, as were stories of genetic abnormalities, curiosities of nature, and industrial and scientific wonders. Executions, Indian attacks, accidents, and deaths were also reported. Not surprisingly, the more bizarre happenings of the revival were also presented by the papers, particularly after 1741. A story of an African American exhorter printed in the *Boston Weekly Post-Boy* on May 17, 1742, although probably fictitious, was not unusual and was eagerly reprinted by the *New-York Weekly Journal* on May 24 and the *American Weekly Mercury* on May 27: "As he was exhorting the People, two large monstrous black Snakes crept up on his Back, and look'd over each of his Shoulders to the great Surprize both of himself and his Audience." Thus, the nature of the revival as presented by the papers after 1741 appeared more controversial, irrational, and dangerous than during Whitefield's first preaching tour.

Just as the nature of the revival appeared differently in newspapers after Whitefield's first tour, so too did the effects of the movement. Until 1741, newspaper reports had emphasized the attentiveness of revival audiences, the increased spirituality of congregations and towns after being visited by revivalist preachers, and the widespread support received by Whitefield and other itinerants. After Whitefield left the colonies, reports and letters in the papers began suggesting that more negative effects might be the by-products of revival.

Many contributors questioned the impact of the revival on colonial social order, as the very order and rules of society appeared vulnerable to revival extremes. For example, in Philadelphia on September 10, 1741, the *American Weekly Mercury* related the story of New Light clergyman the Rev. Cross of Baskin-Ridge, who according to the *Mercury* report, told a virgin who applied to him for counsel that she must be a "very notorious Sinner" to receive salvation. Thus, he had sexual relations with her repeatedly until she conceived, after which he married her to another man, assuring him that she was "blessed."[38] On October 10, 1743, the *Boston Evening-Post* reported that New Light believers in Connecticut, after hearing a revivalist preach that "there was no more Holiness in a Church, than in an Oak Tree," decided to apply the message by "easing themselves in the Church, and defiling it with Ordure in several Places."

Even the institution of marriage appeared to be in jeopardy as enthusiasts strained their spouses' patience or led them into religious fanaticism. The *Boston Weekly Post-Boy* reported on August 16, 1742, that an English weaver who "had the Misfortune of being married to one of Whitefield's S--ts," found his wife giving gold pieces to Whitefield's ministry. He stole the gold back from his wife and used the "Strappado" to break her of her allegiance. The *Boston Evening-Post* reprinted an item from the British *Spectator* in which the writer complained of married life with a "Gospel-gosip" [sic]—she continually attends lectures and meetings, ignores her home responsibilities, and harangues her husband with excerpts from sermons she has heard.[39] The *Boston Weekly Post-Boy* reported on December 15, 1746, that "a noted Person in the Theatrical Way, has lately turn'd Methodist by the Perswasion of his Wife." Both of these reports were reprinted by other colonial newspapers.[40]

After 1741, the papers also printed stories of how the revival was affecting colonial government. Many carried reports of zealots who attempted to influence government policy with their prophecies and predictions, Hugh Bryan of South Carolina being the most famous. Bryan was a South Carolina planter who became a follower of Whitefield, held religious meetings for African Americans, and prophesied destruction for the town of Charleston. On March 27, 1742, the *South-Carolina Gazette* reported that formal charges had been brought against Bryan by Carolina officials, but Bryan repented before he was arrested. Whitefield and the English Methodists were often accused of disloyalty to the king and of holding papal sympathies, particularly after the second Jacobite rebellion of 1745.[41] After the Virginia capitol building burned to the ground, the *Maryland Gazette* for April 14, 1747, recorded the Virginia council's opinion that the fire was "an awful incitement to a reformation of manners," indirectly the result of the "spirit of Enthusiasm introduced among the people by itinerant preachers; a spirit more dangerous to the common welfare than the furious element which laid the Royal edifice in ashes."

The papers also noted government action against the ill effects of the revival. Although the *Boston Weekly News-Letter* had printed Massachusetts' "official" endorsement of the revival on July 17, 1740, by January 14, 1742, the paper was printing Connecticut's warning that the weaknesses of the revival be corrected. Connecticut's law against itinerant preaching was reported by the *Boston Gazette* on June 29, 1742, and New York's law appeared in the *Boston Evening-Post* on March 11, 1745. Virginia Governor William Gooch's charge to the Grand Jury of Virginia was printed on the front page of the *American Weekly Mercury* on August 8, 1745, probably because Gooch's primary subject matter was the condemnation of itinerant preachers who "professing themselves Ministers, under the pretended Influence of New-Light, extraordinary Impulse, and such like fanatical and enthusiastical Knowledge, lead the innocent and ignorant People into all Kinds of Delusion."

Besides the deleterious effects of the revival on the social order of the colonies, reports and letters in the newspapers after 1741 began to suggest that the movement was also affecting the religious order of the colonies in a negative way. Specifically, contributors questioned the revival's influence on the ministerial office, church unity, and orthodox Christian doctrine.

A primary concern expressed in the papers after 1741 was that the revival endangered the honor and integrity of the ministerial office. The threat was seen as coming primarily from the preponderance of lay preachers. As ministers preached the message of the "New Birth," some of their listeners who experienced conversion would themselves feel the call to go and preach. Without formal training and sometimes without even the ability to read, these itinerant preachers would travel the country, preaching to whoever would listen. The December 8, 1743, *Boston Weekly Post-Boy* printed a letter from a New England correspondent to a recipient in London bemoaning the presence of itinerants—"a gifted (or rather conceited) Brother [who] sets up for an Exhorter," causing listeners to "forsake the Houses of their stated Worship and Communion."

The colonial papers printed numerous reports of itinerant lay preachers and the trouble they caused, fueling public fear that these "Pedlars in Divinity" would eventually destroy the pastoral office.[42] Richard Woodbury of Rowley, Massachusetts, was ordained as an itinerant evangelist by revivalist minister Nicholas Gilman in a private ceremony. Woodbury preached vehement sermons and condemned and cursed those who opposed him.[43] Rejected even by most revivalists, the "poor crazy Exhorter" was featured in the Boston papers during the summer of 1744.[44] Nathaniel Wardell, a hay weigher, appeared in the *Boston Evening-Post* on March 21, 1743, when he allegedly baptized two women in the sea, "one of whom, 'tis said, suffer'd pretty much by the Unskillfulness of the Administrator." Even the infamous eighteenth-century confidence man Tom Bell engaged in lay preaching, albeit for different motives than most, the *Boston Evening-Post* reported on September 12, 1743. A report from Providence, Rhode Island, printed in the *Boston Evening-Post* on August 23, 1742, related a near-riot during a revival meeting caused by overzealous "Exhorters," one of whom was reported to have cried to the women in the audience, "Oh! I have had many a d---n'd cursed Frolick amongst your cursed Hoop'd Petticoats!" Vicious debate over itinerancy appeared in the papers, particularly in Boston, as contributors argued the appropriateness of the practice.[45]

Some established ministers added to the controversy when they began leaving their congregations for periods of time to travel as itinerant preachers. Gilbert Tennent, James Davenport, Andrew Croswell, John Moorhead, and others drew sharp criticism for preaching in other men's parishes. Ministers like Davenport, Benjamin Pomeroy, and Samuel Buell attracted even more negative attention because of their unorthodox practices of singing in public streets and criticizing other ministers. A report in the *Boston Weekly Post-Boy* on April 5, 1742,

questioned the appropriateness and motives of Samuel Buell's followers in Boston as they "march'd up from the Ferry thro' the main-Streets
of the Town singing of Hymns."

Some colonies outlawed itinerant and lay preaching, hoping to stop
parishioners from criticizing their pastors. Both Connecticut and New
York passed laws against itinerancy. In a speech reprinted by the *New-
York Evening-Post* on February 22, 1747, Governor William Shirley of
Massachusetts encouraged lawmakers to ensure adequate salaries for
ministers to avoid the "great Danger of the Pulpits being filled with ignorant and illiterate Men, and all manner of foolish and hurtful Errors being
thereby propagated." Ministers did not help their own standing by what
many saw as their constant bickering in the public newspapers. In a letter
contributed to the *Boston Evening-Post* by "Jeremiah Layman" on January 24, 1743, the author argued that respect for ministers in Boston was
at an all-time low and criticized ministers for appearing in the papers.

Church unity appeared to also be threatened by the revival, as
newspapers printed reports of church conflicts and splits, a practice
more often seen in New England than elsewhere in the colonies. Christopher Grasso has written that between 1742 and 1745, Connecticut
experienced nineteen church separations, while Massachusetts endured
thirteen. By 1750, forty separations had occurred in Connecticut and
thirty-seven in Massachusetts.[46] The Boston papers carried news of
church splits regularly, sometimes making an explicit connection with
itinerant preaching. The *Boston Weekly News-Letter* (March 8, 1744)
and *Boston Evening-Post* (March 12) reported on the Rev. Ezra Carpenter's arguments over the revival with the congregation of the First
Congregational Church in Hull, Massachusetts. As the *Post* reported
it: "The Town of Hull having for a long Time been disturbed by the
preaching and exhorting of some rambling and turbulent Zealots, a
Number of the People were so far prejudiced against their Rev. and
worthy Pastor, as to leave his Ministry, and exhibited Fifteen Articles
of Charge against him relating to Errors in Doctrine." Carpenter was
exonerated by an ecclesiastical council, but was ultimately dismissed in
November 1746. On September 16, 1746, the *Boston Gazette* reported
on a member of revivalist Daniel Bliss' church in Concord, Massachusetts, who objected to Bliss' encouragement of separatists in Boston.
On May 3, 1742, the *Boston Evening-Post* reported on the struggles of

the Rev. Christopher Toppan of Newbury, Massachusetts, with itinerant preachers; by March 31, 1746, the *Post* reported that disaffected members from Toppan's church had officially formed a new congregation and called revivalist Jonathan Parsons of Lyme, Connecticut, as their pastor. The Rev. Theophilus Pickering printed an open letter against itinerant Ebenezar Cleaveland on March 18, 1746, in the *Boston Gazette*, but Awakening sympathizers from Pickering's parish eventually left and formed a new church under Ebenezar's brother John Cleaveland in 1747.

Many contributors to the papers blamed the church splits not only on itinerant preaching, but also on the censorious nature of those favoring the revival. An article reprinted from Benjamin Franklin's *General Magazine* in the *Boston Weekly Post-Boy* for August 17, 1741, presents a "Recipe to make a new Kind of a Convert." Ingredients include "Spirits of Pride;" "Roots of Obstinacy, Ignorance and Controversy;" and the "Water of Strife."[47] To be fair, opponents of the revival were often as judgmental as were the revivalists. On February 15 and February 22, 1742, the *New-York Weekly Journal* printed an excerpt from Richard Hooker's London paper the *Weekly Miscellany* which condemned Whitefield, John Wesley, and the Methodists. On March 8, the *Journal* printed a contributed excerpt from Lord Molesworth which encouraged religious tolerance among "Pagans, Turks, Jews, Papists, Quakers, Socinians, Presbyterians, or others."[48] Some ministers resigned from their churches because of differences of opinion with members over the revival. On August 17, 1741, the *Boston Evening-Post* reported that in "many Towns," the "Disposition and Management of the People, as well as these evangelizing Gentlemen [itinerant preachers], has been accounted so irregular and disorderly, by some pious, learned and worthy Ministers, that if the Disorders continue, they are resolved to ask a Dismission from their respective Churches."

Lastly, contributors to the papers worried that orthodox doctrine would be adversely affected by the revival. Both revivalists and their opponents contributed excerpts to the papers from past clergymen and writers affirming or refuting doctrines associated with the revival. Samuel Butler (1612-1680), Richard Baxter (1615-1691), Matthew Prior (1664-1721), Cotton Mather (1663-1728), John Milton (1608-1674), and Matthew Henry (1662-1714) all appeared in excerpt form in the papers to argue for one side or the other.[49] Revivalists often attempted to prove that the revival was returning American Christianity to the theology of the early church, while opponents claimed the revival depended too much on personal religious impulses and not enough on conventional church doctrine. The revival in America was strongly Calvinistic, a theological system which emphasizes God's sovereignty in human affairs. Original sin, the belief that Adam's guilt was imputed to the entire human race, was key to the revivalist concept of the New Birth. If one is not inherently sinful, one does not need to be saved by a sovereign, gracious God. Letters in the colonial papers attacked and defended original sin, the most notable argument carried by the *South-Carolina Gazette* from January 1740 through January 1741 between the Rev. Josiah Smith and the Anglican Commissary Alexander Garden.[50] Other orthodox Christian doctrines such as the existence of heaven and hell were also discussed in the newspapers.[51]

A primary concern for opponents was the revivalist emphasis on salvation by God's grace alone. The vast majority of revivalists adhered to the Reformation doctrine of *sola gratia*, the belief that man's eternal salvation is given as a gift by God, not earned by human good works. Revival supporters were often attacked in the papers as antinomians, or those "against the law," and many critics claimed revivalists discouraged obedience to biblical laws. On December 3, 1744, the *Boston Evening-Post* carried a letter from J. F. criticizing what the writer believed was Whitefield's antinomianism. Only a few months later on May 27, 1745, the *Post* printed another letter attacking Whitefield as an antinomianist, this time by a gentleman in London "who has had favourable Thoughts of Mr. Whitefield." Even the revivalists themselves worried about unorthodoxy in their midst. In the April 15, 1742, *Boston Weekly News-Letter*, Gilbert Tennent criticized the American Moravians, supporters of the Awakening and followers of Count Zinzendorf, for what he viewed as their "confused Medly [sic] of rank Antinomianism and Quakerism." In September 1745, Boston ministers attempted to bring doctrinal cohesion to the Awakening by publishing a testimony recommending the Westminster Confession of Faith.[52]

By 1746, coverage of the Awakening decreased significantly—while 1745 had seen 199 items printed on the revival, 1746 saw only 104. Only 115 items appeared in 1747, and 71 items appeared in 1748, when Whitefield finished his second preaching tour and left the colonies.

By 1746, news reports returned to outnumbering letters, and coverage overall returned to being mostly positive or neutral. These patterns continued through 1748. Whitefield's more conciliatory approach certainly influenced this development, as did a public recantation and apology by James Davenport, and published doubts about the movement by Gilbert Tennent.

Franklin continued to follow Whitefield's movements closely throughout 1747 as the evangelist made his final travels through the Middle Colonies and New England. Franklin reprinted reports on Whitefield from papers in Boston, New York, and South Carolina, updating his readers on Whitefield's preaching stops.[53] Franklin also printed a report on Gilbert Tennent on December 29, 1747, when he preached in the New Building in Philadelphia erected for Whitefield. Little commentary on the revival or its main participants was seen in Franklin's *Gazette* during the last years of Whitefield's second preaching tour, as Franklin printed no letters discussing the Awakening in 1747 or 1748 and only one letter in 1746, revealing the decrease in public discussion of the movement. Franklin did, however, use his *Gazette* to defend Whitefield on April 23, 1747. After reprinting a letter from the Rev. Josiah Smith in Charleston, South Carolina, which attested to Whitefield's place of esteem among gentlemen of "Distinction and Substance," Franklin added his own closing comment regarding Whitefield's honesty, designed to defend the evangelist against charges that he improperly used ministry donations. The item was reprinted by the *Pennsylvania Journal* (April 24) and the *New-York Gazette* (April 27). Franklin reported on Whitefield as he left Charleston, preached in Bermuda, and arrived in Edinburgh for a preaching stop in 1748. He also reported on the first commencement exercises at the New Light College of New Jersey (later Princeton). Franklin's consistent coverage of the Awakening in his *Pennsylvania Gazette* reveals how colonial printers throughout the colonies enabled readers to corporately experience the religious events and issues of the 1740s.

An innkeeper in North Carolina, a farmer in Connecticut, a printer in Philadelphia—each experienced the force of the revival personally, but also corporately as they followed the movement through their local newspapers. As one of the primary vehicles for communicating ideas and emotions about the religious events of the 1740s, the colonial newspapers presented to readers one "version" of the American revival—a movement that, according to the papers, was widespread and volatile. During years of coverage, different aspects and effects of the movement were emphasized by the papers, yet the story always remained central to newspapers during the 1740s. It is no wonder that Benjamin Franklin recalled years later in his autobiography: "[I]t seem'd as if all the World were growing Religious."[54]

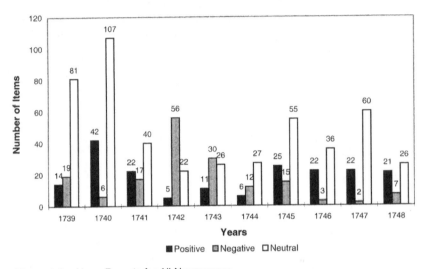

Figure 1.1. *News Reports for All Newspapers*

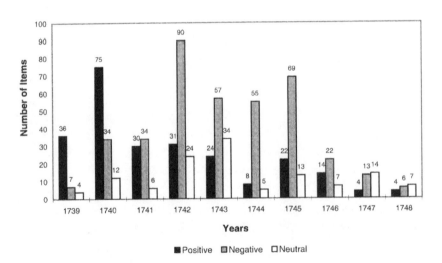

Figure 1.2. *Letters for All Newspapers*

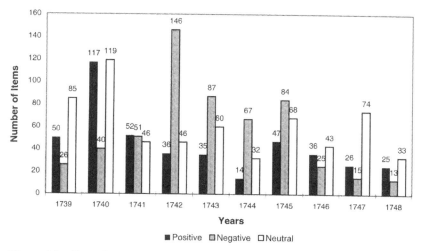

Figure 1.3.   *News Reports and Letters for All Newspapers*

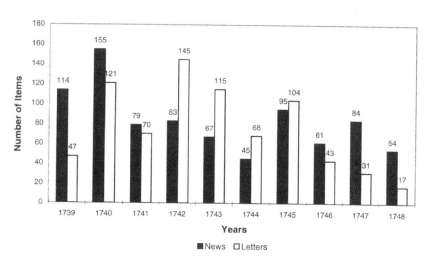

Figure 1.4.   *News Reports versus Letters for All Newspapers*

NOTES

1. Excerpted from Darrett B. Rutman, *The Great Awakening: Event and Exegesis* (New York: John Wiley & Sons, 1970), 44.

2. George Whitefield, *George Whitefield's Journals* (Carlisle, PA: Banner of Truth Trust, 1960), 373. All quotations from Whitefield's journals are from

Banner of Truth Trust's 6th edition. Further citations to this work are given in the text.

3. Lambert, *Inventing*, 108.

4. Richard D. Brown, *Knowledge is Power: The Diffusion of Information in Early America, 1700-1865* (New York: Oxford University Press, 1989), 139.

5. Excerpted from David S. Lovejoy, *Religious Enthusiasm and the Great Awakening*, American Historical Sources Series (Englewood Cliffs, NJ: Prentice-Hall, 1969), 42-43.

6. The *Boston Evening-Post* accounted for 256, or 46 percent, of the negative items.

7. The German paper *Der Hoch-Deutsch Pennsylvänische Geschickt-Schrieber* was printed in Germantown, Pennsylvania, from 1739 to 1746, but is not discussed in this book.

8. Clark, *Public Prints*, 194-99. See Lawrence C. Wroth, *The Colonial Printer* (1938; repr. New York: Dover, 1994) and Hugh Amory and David D. Hall, eds., *A History of the Book in America: The Colonial Book in the Atlantic World* (Cambridge, MA: Cambridge University Press, 2000), for background on colonial printing in general.

9. See Clark, *Public Prints*, 200-207, for more detail on the cost of and requirements for printing a newspaper. See also Frank Luther Mott, *American Journalism, A History: 1690-1960*, 3rd ed. (New York: Macmillan, 1962), 43-48, and Wroth, *Colonial Printer*.

10. Clark, *Public Prints*, 205-6.

11. See Copeland, *Colonial American Newspapers*, Appendix 2, for a content breakdown of selected colonial newspapers.

12. Clark, *Public Prints*, 259. Printers were dependent upon the colonial postal service for delivery of their newspapers. Postmasters who also published newspapers often used their mail privileges to thwart the delivery of rival papers. See Isaiah Thomas, *The History of Printing in America* (1810; repr., Barre, Massachusetts: Imprint Society, 1970), 454, for a note regarding Pennsylvania's postal service, and both Wallace B. Eberhard, "Press and Post Office in Eighteenth-Century America: Origins of a Public Policy," in *Newsletters to Newspapers: Eighteenth-Century Journalism* (Morgantown, West Virginia: The School of Journalism, West Virginia University, 1977), and Mott, *American Journalism*, 60-63, for short discussions of the relationship between colonial newspapers and the postal service.

13. Marilyn J. Westerkamp, "Enthusiastic Piety—From Scots-Irish Revivals to the Great Awakening," in *Belief and Behavior: Essays in the New Religious History*, eds. Philip R. Vandermeer and Robert P. Swierenga, 63-87 (New Brunswick, NJ: Rutgers University Press, 1991), 67.

14. Jon Butler was the first to offer this revisionist understanding of the Awakening by asserting that the movement missed most colonies and is difficult to date accurately. Harry S. Stout's biography of Whitefield considers how the evangelist exploited the emerging consumer culture to strengthen and popularize himself and his message. Frank Lambert has shown how eighteenth-century revivalists used print and oral media to "invent" the Great Awakening and present it to readers as a sweeping, powerful work of God.

15. The reprints appeared in the *Boston Evening-Post* (November 11), *New England Weekly Journal* (November 20), and *Boston Weekly News-Letter* (November 22).

16. The reprints appeared in the *American Weekly Mercury* (March 4) and *Pennsylvania Gazette* (March 6) in Philadelphia, the *New-York Weekly Journal* (March 10) in New York, and the *New England Weekly Journal* (March 25) in Boston.

17. Reprints from English papers were not counted as reprints the first time they appeared in American papers. When two papers in the same city printed the exact same news report on the same day, one of the printings was counted as a reprint.

18. Also included in this number are contributed poems and excerpts from published works. The vast majority, however, were original letters written and contributed by readers.

19. See the *Boston Weekly Post-Boy*, January 12, 1741, and the *Boston Weekly News-Letter*, April 15, 1742, for the negative letters.

20. For reprinted notices, see the *Pennsylvania Gazette* for January 15 and February 19, 1741.

21. For the letters, see September 2 (2), October 21, and December 8 (2) (Postscript), 1742.

22. *Boston Weekly News-Letter*, November 13, 1741.

23. Benjamin Franklin's appreciation of Whitefield can be found in Leonard W. Labaree, ed. *The Papers of Benjamin Franklin*, vol. 2 (New Haven, CT: Yale University Press, 1959), 287-88. The dates for the reprinting are *Boston Gazette* (June 23, 1740), *Boston Weekly Post-Boy* (June 23), *New England Weekly Journal* (June 24), *Boston Weekly News-Letter* (June 26); and *South-Carolina Gazette* (July 25).

24. Fifty-seven of the negative items appeared in the *Boston Evening-Post*.

25. Milton J. Coalter, Jr., *Gilbert Tennent, Son of Thunder: A Case Study of Continental Pietism's Impact on the First Great Awakening in the Middle Colonies*, Contributions to the Study of Religion 18 (New York: Greenwood Press, 1986), 82-85; Leonard J. Trinterud, *The Forming of an American Tradition: A Re-examination of Colonial Presbyterianism* (1949: repr. Freeport,

NY: Books for Libraries Press, 1970), 103-8. The revivalist ministers created the Londonderry Presbytery and joined it to the old New Brunswick Presbytery to create their Synod, with the New York Presbytery joining in 1745 (Rutman, *Event and Exegesis*, 173). The factions formally reunited in 1758 (see Coalter, *Gilbert Tennent*, 155-56).

26. See Coalter, *Gilbert Tennent*, 85-88, for more detail.

27. At the next annual meeting of the synod in May 1742, moderate revivalist Jonathan Dickinson was elected moderator and attempted to reconcile the warring factions. Unsuccessful, Dickinson and nine others formally protested to the synod, denouncing the synod's treatment of the excluded members, but the synod took no action. On August 12, 1742, Dickinson's protestation appeared in the *Pennsylvania Gazette*, complaining of the exclusion of the members of the New Brunswick Presbytery from the Philadelphia Synod and proclaiming the revival a "Work of Divine Power and Grace" (Coalter, *Gilbert Tennent*, 106-7).

28. See the *Boston Weekly News-Letter*, June 10, 1742, for Connecticut, and September 2, 1742, for Massachusetts.

29. See the *Boston Weekly Post-Boy*, May 24, 1742, and the *Boston Evening-Post*, June 14, 1742.

30. See the *Pennsylvania Gazette* for September 2 (2), October 21, and December 8 Postscript (2), 1742, for the letters.

31. For the reprints, see the *Boston Weekly News-Letter*, Sept. 23, 1742; *Boston Evening-Post*, September 27, 1742; *Boston Evening-Post*, October 11, 1742; *Boston Evening-Post*, November 8, 1742; and *South-Carolina Gazette*, March 14, 1743.

32. Additional appearances of the Shepherd's Tent in colonial newspapers can be found in the *Boston Evening-Post*, September 13, 1742; *Boston Weekly Post-Boy*, November 8, 1742; and *Boston Evening-Post*, March 28, 1743.

33. *Boston Evening-Post*, October 15, 1744.

34. For more on religious enthusiasm, see David S. Lovejoy, *Religious Enthusiasm in the New World* (Cambridge, MA: Harvard University Press, 1985) and Leigh Eric Schmidt, *Hearing Things: Religion, Illusion, and the American Enlightenment* (Cambridge, MA: Harvard University Press, 2000), 192ff.

35. Garden later authored *A Brief Account of the Deluded Dutartes* (New Haven, 1762).

36. See the *Boston Evening-Post*, November 10, 1740; *South-Carolina Gazette*, May 14, 1741; *Boston Gazette*, January 26, 1748; and *Boston Weekly News-Letter*, February 18, 1748.

37. See the *Pennsylvania Gazette*, October 16, 1740, which notes that the letter containing the story of the Boston tragedy is a reprint from the *New-York*

Gazette for October 13, 1740 (not extant). See the *Boston Evening-Post*, September 29, 1740; *New England Weekly Journal*, September 23, 1740; *Boston Weekly News-Letter*, September 25, 1740; and *Boston Gazette*, September 29, 1740.

38. Although the truth of the story cannot be determined, Cross was suspended by his presbytery on June 23, 1742, and not reinstated (Richard Webster, *A History of the Presbyterian Church in America* [Philadelphia, PA: Joseph M. Wilson, 1857], 413-14).

39. January 14, 1745. The piece is from *The Spectator*, April 23, 1711, no. 46, and was the magazine's first reference to the Quakers. In its use here, however, it obviously is designed to attack followers of Whitefield and the Awakening.

40. The article from the *Boston Evening-Post* was reprinted by the *South-Carolina Gazette* on January 6, 1746, and the article from the *Boston Weekly Post-Boy* was reprinted by the *Boston Weekly News-Letter* on December 18, 1746. See also the *Boston Evening-Post*, May 9, 1743, and the *New-York Weekly Post-Boy*, November 24, 1746, for additional comments on marriage and the revival. See Harry S. Stout, *The Divine Dramatist: George Whitefield and the Rise of Modern Evangelicalism,* Library of Religious Biography (Grand Rapids, MI: Wm. B. Eerdmans, 1991), 156-73, for a discussion of Whitefield's view of women in ministry, and see Susan Juster, *Disorderly Women: Sexual Politics and Evangelicalism in Revolutionary New England* (Ithaca, NY: Cornell University Press, 1994), for some insights into women and the revival.

41. For government policy, see the *Boston Gazette*, November 5, 1739; for Hugh Bryan, see the *South-Carolina Gazette*, March 6, 1742; for the Jacobite Rebellion, see the *Boston Evening-Post*, March 30, 1747, and the *Boston Gazette*, March 31, 1747.

42. The term is from the *Boston Weekly News-Letter*, April 22, 1742.

43. Joseph Tracy, *The Great Awakening: A History of the Revival of Religion in the Time of Edwards and Whitefield* (1841; repr., New York: Arno Press, 1969), 335-36.

44. See the *Boston Gazette*, July 24, 1744, and the *Boston Evening-Post*, August 6, 1744.

45. See the *Boston Weekly News-Letter*, October 28, 1742, and the *Boston Gazette*, November 30, 1742, for letters from one such debate.

46. Christopher A Grasso, *Speaking Aristocracy: Transforming Public Discourse in Eighteenth-Century Connecticut* (Chapel Hill, NC: Omohundro Institute of Early American History and Culture / University of North Carolina Press, 1999), 104.

47. See also the *Boston Evening-Post*, March 22, 1742; *Boston Gazette*, January 4, 1743; *Boston Evening-Post*, January 30, 1744; and *Boston Evening-Post*, March 12, 1744.

48. The author could be Robert Molesworth, first Viscount Molesworth (1656-1725), an English politician, writer, and member of the Royal Society (*Dictionary of National Biography: From the Earliest Times to 1900*, 66 vols. in 22. [London: Oxford University Press, 1921-1922], 13:568-70).

49. For Butler, see *South-Carolina Gazette*, August 8, 1740; for Baxter, *Boston Weekly News-Letter*, December 23, 1742; for Prior, *South-Carolina Gazette*, August 23, 1740; for Mather, *Boston Weekly News-Letter*, November 18, 1742; for Milton, *South-Carolina Gazette*, February 9, 1740, and following issues; for Henry, *Boston Gazette*, December 11, 1744.

50. See chapter 2 for a complete discussion of this paper war.

51. See, for example, the *Boston Evening-Post*, March 15, 1742.

52. The meeting to write the statement was advertised in the *Boston Gazette* on May 28, 1745.

53. For example, see the *Pennsylvania Gazette* for March 10 (*Boston Gazette* February 3 reprint), July 2 (*New-York Gazette* June 29 reprint), and November 19 (*South-Carolina Gazette* October 26 reprint), all for 1747.

54. J. A. Leo Lemay and P. M. Zall, *The Autobiography of Benjamin Franklin: A Genetic Text* (Knoxville: University of Tennessee Press, 1981), 103.

CHAPTER 2

Regional Paper Wars

Tho' I live at some Distance from your Town, (which of late has been the Seat of Paper War) yet I have carefully perus'd the Papers and Pamphlets as they have come out, concerning the Times.

Boston Evening-Post, June 3, 1745

It is very pleasant to find that Envy and Prejudice against him [Whitefield] here, except from those who don't agree with him in Doctrine, does not prevail with that Bitterness as from many in your Country.

Letter from Bristol, England, to a recipient in Boston, 1748[1]

When disagreement over the Awakening split the Philadelphia Synod of the Presbyterian denomination in the summer of 1741, printer Benjamin Franklin was quick to report the event in his *Pennsylvania Gazette* for June 11. In a paragraph, Franklin reported that revival supporters had been "excluded" from the synod and removed themselves to another meeting place. One would expect that such an event would be reprinted by newspapers in all the colonies, but, in fact, the split was heavily reprinted in some, but not at all in others. In Boston, the *Boston Gazette, Boston Weekly Post-Boy*, and *New England Weekly Journal* reprinted the story, with the *Post-Boy* reprinting a follow-up item from the *Philadelphia Gazette* a few weeks later. In Charleston, printer Elizabeth Timothy reprinted the report in the *South-Carolina Gazette*. Neither of the newspapers publishing in New York reprinted Franklin's report.[2]

When the Rev. Gilbert Tennent, one of the foremost colonial re-vivalists during the Awakening, wrote a letter to a friend questioning the movement and his own involvement in it, *Boston Weekly News-Letter* printer John Draper published the letter in his paper on July 22, 1742. The letter was quickly reprinted by the *Boston Evening-Post* (July 26), the *American Weekly Mercury* and *Pennsylvania Gazette* in Philadelphia (August 12), and the *South-Carolina Gazette* (December 6). No New York paper reprinted Tennent's confession.[3] When Ten-nent sent an explanatory letter to Benjamin Franklin to print in his September 2 *Pennsylvania Gazette,* both the *Boston Weekly News-Letter* (September 23) and the *Boston Evening-Post* (September 27) reprinted that letter.

The reprint histories of both the synod split and Gilbert Tennent's letters reveal that while the basic characteristics of the Awakening emphasized in the papers did not differ significantly from paper to paper or from region to region, as shown in the previous chapter, but transformed over time, contributed letters were unique to each news-paper and region and caused local print battles that often were not reported in other parts of the colonies. These regional "paper wars," as these disputes were often called, differed in terms of what contributors argued about and the manner in which they battled. These local paper wars, then, most clearly reveal the principal controversies and concerns regarding the Awakening in each region of the colonies.

Several factors account for the way the newspapers in each region handled controversies related to the revival. One factor was simply the number of available newspapers in each city. Some areas of the country boasted several weekly newspapers, while other colonies pro-duced only one. Six papers were printed in Boston during the 1740s, New York enjoyed four, and Philadelphians had three from which to choose. Annapolis, Williamsburg, and Charleston each had only one paper. Multiple papers provided multiple perspectives, as well as more frequent and expansive coverage. Numerous newspapers and a strong reader base also enabled "party papers" to survive; Samuel Kneeland and Timothy Green Jr.'s *Boston Gazette* unabashedly supported the re-vival, while Thomas Fleet's *Boston Evening-Post* consistently attacked it. Papers such as the *South-Carolina Gazette* and *Maryland Gazette* could not afford to be so partial.

In addition, as scholars have noted, some regions of the country were more prepared for revival than were others, and their papers thus covered revival happenings more closely and argued more intensely over the merits of the movement. The "revival districts" of the Connecticut Valley of New England and the Raritan Valley of eastern New Jersey expected "outpourings" of God's grace and thus responded more positively to Whitefield and the New Lights.[4] Papers in New England and Philadelphia printed by far the most reports on the revival—885 and 376 notices, respectively, during the years 1739 through 1748. New York, on the other hand, despite producing four weekly newspapers, did not have such a history of revival and printed only a total of 157 revival-related items. Figure 2.1 reveals the disparity in amount of coverage of the Awakening (see figures at the end of this chapter).

Another influence on regional newspaper coverage of revival-related controversies was the attitudes of the printers themselves toward the events.[5] Since each newspaper printer made the majority of the editorial decisions for his paper, his influence was significant. Deciding which news items and letters to print was the purview of the colonial printer. For example, in Boston, Thomas Fleet established himself as a staunch opponent of Whitefield and the Awakening; the fact that Fleet printed almost 50 percent of the negative letters that appeared in the papers across the colonies during Whitefield's first two colonial preaching tours reveals the influence a printer could have. On the other hand, William Bradford's announcement in his *New-York Gazette* on January 22, 1740, that he would no longer "incert [sic] any more of these Controversies" related to the Awakening in his newspaper certainly influenced how much information *Gazette* readers received about the revival. *South-Carolina Gazette* printer Elizabeth Timothy's position as one of Franklin's long-distance printing partners ensured that she would receive and print information from the Middle Colonies such as the report of the Presbyterian Synod split.

Lastly, reader preference and interest influenced how different papers covered the Awakening. In Massachusetts, where clergymen made up 70 percent of the learned professionals in the colony in 1740,[6] debate over the Awakening was strong and consistent. In South Carolina, the presence of the Rev. Josiah Smith ensured that the revival held a prominent place in the papers as he consistently contributed letters to the *South-Carolina Gazette* that discussed theological issues raised by the Awakening as well as reports from various revivalists.

The paper wars of the revival constituted a large percentage of the newspaper coverage of the movement. Of the 1598 newspaper items related to the revival printed in the papers between 1739 and 1748, 761 were letters (48 percent).[7] Only 17 percent of the letters were neutral (126), usually discussing points of Christian doctrine related to the revival or asking other contributors to cease quarreling. Most letters were either positive or negative toward the movement; specifically, 33 percent of the letters were positive (248) while 51 percent were negative (387).[8] The three most recognized revivalists—George Whitefield (46 percent), Gilbert Tennent (7 percent), and James Davenport (6 percent)—were the subjects or authors of almost 60 percent of all letters. Letters even accounted for 30 percent of all reprints. The abundance of contributed letters assured that nearly half of what the public read in the colonial newspapers about the revival was opinion, not news.

It was during the years of the most intense debate over the revival that letters outnumbered news items in the papers. Specifically, these years were those after Whitefield's first preaching tour and during the beginning of his second tour, 1742 through 1745. The most letters for one year appeared in 1742 (145), when Whitefield had finished his explosive first tour and numerous native revivalists had begun to travel the colonies themselves, repeating his message. Scholars have long noted the significance and intensity of the public print debate regarding the Awakening.[9] Contributed letters in the newspapers were a significant part of that discussion.

By printing contributed letters, the papers functioned as a place in which readers could do more than just read about important happenings—they could also discuss those events and their meaning. Newspapers were the perfect vehicle for debate, for while discussions in taverns and coffeehouses were limited to those present, newspaper disputes could involve all who read the papers. During the 1740s, this virtual debate space functioned as a public arena for dialogue and argument regarding topics as diverse as ministers' salaries, itinerant preaching, the doctrine of original sin, and, of course, the actions and opinions of well-known revivalists such as Whitefield and Tennent. No other topic in the early eighteenth century received so much newspaper debate as did the Awakening. These paper wars were carried on through letters contributed to the papers, the letters usually appearing on the front page and written by both clergymen and laymen, sometimes drawing the printers themselves into the disputes. Even a casual reader of colonial newspapers in the 1740s would have noted the preponderance of disputation and discussion regarding religious events. As seven Boston ministers remarked in 1742 in an attestation attached to Jonathan Dickinson's *A Display of God's Special Grace*, "He must be a Stranger in Israel, who has not heard of the uncommon religious Appearances in the several Parts of this Land, among Persons of all Ages and Characters. This is an Affair which has in some Degree drawn every One's Attention, and been the Subject of much Debate both in Conversation and Writing." The debate in conversation took place in the churches and coffeehouses, while the debate in writing took place primarily through pamphlets and the local newspapers.

Local controversies made up approximately 40 percent of all contributed letters during Whitefield's first two preaching tours.[10] Parts of these conflicts were at times reprinted by papers in other regions, but most remained local in their appeal. This chapter will examine how the newspapers in each region of the colonies dealt with religious disagreement during the 1740s by examining the principal local paper wars—the topics discussed, the style of argument, and the characteristics of the debates.

NEW ENGLAND: BOSTON

Newspapers in Boston followed the revival very closely, which is not surprising based on the religious and printing heritage of New England. Religiously, New England's Puritan tradition was still strong at the time of Whitefield's visits, despite cycles of growth and decline in church interest and involvement over the decades. Periodic religious revivals were expected and encouraged by ministers throughout New England. Smaller revivals such as the 1734/1735 revival in Jonathan Edwards' church in Northampton, Massachusetts, had prepared New Englanders to expect a divine move of God at any time.[11]

Printing, like religion, was well-established in New England by the time of the Awakening. The first presses in the colonies had begun in Massachusetts, and historian and printer Isaiah Thomas notes that before 1740, more printing was done in that colony than in all other colonies combined.[12] Newspapers began in Boston almost fifteen years before they appeared in the other colonies, and by the time of Whitefield's arrival in 1739, five weekly newspapers were publishing in Boston.

Thus, the strength of both the religious and print cultures in this region led to very close coverage of Whitefield and the revival by Boston newspapers. In fact, the first characteristic of note regarding reporting in Boston on the religious events of the decade is the frequency and volume of reporting. During the years spanning Whitefield's first two preaching tours of the colonies, 1739-1748, the six Boston newspapers printed 885 revival-related items, more than half the total number of revival-related items printed in the colonies as a whole during those years.[13] Figure 2.2 illustrates the significant number of items printed by Boston papers and the tone of the items. Boston papers began reporting on Whitefield while the evangelist was still in England and followed him closely once he arrived in the colonies for his first preaching tour in October 1739. Although Whitefield did not visit New England until September 1740, the Boston papers printed almost twice as many items on Whitefield and the revival in 1739 and 1740 than did newspapers in any other region of the country. In fact, Boston papers followed revival news so closely during Whitefield's first two tours that they reprinted 189 items from other colonial papers, the most reprints by papers in any region of the colonies. Most of the reprints focused on reports of Whitefield's preaching travels. Yet, despite the large number of reprints, the wealth of original reporting in Boston meant that reprints accounted for only 21 percent of all items on the revival in Boston papers, the lowest reprint percentage in the colonies.[14] Boston papers had their original items reprinted by other papers 207 times, making Boston articles the most reprinted in the colonies. Figure 2.3 illustrates the differences in reprint percentages in the various regions of the colonies.

Bostonians' interest in the religious events of the 1740s also helped give Boston the distinction of producing the only colonial magazine devoted solely to the revival—a weekly serial titled *The Christian His-*

tory. Begun on March 5, 1743, the *Christian History* appeared every Saturday for two years and was published by Thomas Prince, Jr., the son of the Rev. Thomas Prince, Sr., of the Old South Church in Boston, a strong revival supporter and probably the main force behind the magazine. Printers Kneeland and Green printed the magazine for Prince.

The *Christian History* was modeled on revival magazines such as Whitefield's *Weekly History* in London and William Macculloch's *Glasgow Weekly History* in Scotland. Most issues of the *Christian History* contained a single revival or conversion narrative from a New England pastor, although sometimes a congregation in the Middle Colonies was featured, along with news of the revival from abroad. An occasional history of an earlier revival also appeared in the magazine. The *Christian History* thus served to broadcast news of the current revival as well as place the movement in a historical and international perspective.[15] Of the twenty-three revival narratives Michael J. Crawford has counted as published in the colonies between 1741 and 1745, all but one were published in the *Christian History*.[16]

News regarding the *Christian History* appeared in Boston newspapers seventeen times during the magazine's two-year run. All but two of those appearances were in Thomas Fleet's *Boston Evening-Post* and were not complimentary.[17] On March 7, 1743, the *Boston Evening-Post* reported on the appearance of the *Christian History* as well as another magazine titled the *Boston Weekly Magazine*. The *Post* noted that while the *Boston Weekly Magazine* appeared to offer "Room for Disputes on both Sides," the *Christian History* seemed to be "a Party Paper, and design'd only for the Use of Special Friends." Apparently, Fleet did not consider himself one of the "Special Friends," as the *Post* attacked the *History* the very next week on March 14 with a satiric letter which remarked that the "Separatists" now had something to read since they held the Bible in such low esteem. The *Post* printed eleven more letters criticizing the *History* for such things as focusing on minute conversion details, deceiving the public, and perpetuating a "Spirit of Enthusiasm and Division in the Land."[18] Fleet himself criticized Prince, Jr., for his magazine's "Tendency to create Animosity and Contention among Mankind" in the May 30, 1743, issue of the *Post*. Supporters of the *Christian History* did not respond to criticisms in the papers, but they did use the *Boston Gazette* on June 28, 1743, to advertise for documented stories of spiritual conversion in connection with the revival.

The *Christian History* ended on February 23, 1745. On March 25, the *Post* printed a contributed piece on the "death" of the magazine, noting the magazine was "of a very weakly Constitution from its Birth," but also remarking that "some ill-natured Strokes in your Paper [Fleet's *Boston Evening-Post*], may, perhaps, have hastned [sic] its Dissolution." Although Thomas Prince, Jr., planned to enter the ministry, he died of consumption in 1748.[19] That the *Christian History* lasted two years is evidence of the interest the reading public of Boston and elsewhere in the colonies had in the Awakening. The first colonial magazines were begun in the 1740s, and of the five that appeared that decade, only two lasted beyond a handful of issues.[20] Only the *Christian History* and the *American Magazine and Historical Chronicle*, printed by Rogers and Fowle and edited by Boston lawyer Jeremiah Gridley, lasted beyond six months, with the *American Magazine* running from September 1743 until December 1746. The next colonial magazine to run longer than one year, William Bradford's *American Magazine and Monthly Chronicle* of Philadelphia, did not appear for another decade.[21]

Besides being frequent, reporting on the Awakening in Boston was also varied—more varied, in fact, than in any other region of the country. Because Boston boasted the most newspapers in the 1740s, coverage of the revival ranged from neutral to outright positive or negative. For example, both the *Boston Weekly News-Letter*, published by John Draper, and the *Boston Weekly Post-Boy*, published by Ellis Huske, were primarily neutral in their approach to reporting on the Awakening. Draper was a deeply religious man and a member of the Brattle Street Church in Boston, which was pastored by Benjamin Colman, a supporter of the revival. Almost half of Draper's imprints were religious in nature, and he increased religious coverage of the *News-Letter* upon becoming publisher. However, during the 1740s, Draper printed works by both revivalists and opponents, and his coverage of the revival in his *News-Letter* was close but primarily impartial. During the years 1739-1748, Draper's *News-Letter* printed 136 revival-related notices, less than the *Boston Evening-Post* and the *Boston Gazette*, but significantly more than the other two Boston papers. Split almost evenly between news items and contributed letters, almost half of his notices of the revival were neutral in tone, while the rest were fairly evenly split between positive and negative. His coverage of the movement decreased significantly after 1742.[22] Similarly, Huske printed eighty-eight revival-related items in his *Boston Weekly Post-Boy* with almost equal numbers of news reports and letters. Huske's coverage was predominantly neutral as well, and almost half of his items appeared in 1742, the year of the most controversy surrounding the revival. After that year, his coverage also decreased significantly.[23] Reprints accounted for almost 30 percent of Draper's printing on the Awakening and almost 25 percent of Huske's. Reprints from Draper's and Huske's papers appeared twenty-seven and twenty-eight times, respectively, during those years.

Taking a decidedly supportive approach to Whitefield and his followers were Samuel Kneeland and Timothy Green Jr., printers of both the *New England Weekly Journal* and the *Boston Gazette*. A member of both a Boston printing empire and of Boston's Old South Church, whose pastor, Thomas Prince, Sr., strongly supported Whitefield and the revival, Kneeland was known for printing religious texts and during the 1740s printed many works for revivalists such as Whitefield, Gilbert Tennent, Jonathan Edwards, and Jonathan Dickinson. His cousin Timothy Green, Jr., joined him in printing the *New England Weekly Journal*, which offered 104 items on the Awakening from 1739 to 1741, only four of which were negative. Kneeland and Green also printed the *Boston Gazette* for the benefit of former publisher John Boydell's widow, assuming proprietorship of the *Gazette* and merging it with the *New England Weekly Journal* in October 1741 to form the *Boston Gazette, or New England Weekly Journal*. Kneeland and Green used the newly formed *Boston Gazette* to advocate the revival as strongly as they had used the *Weekly Journal*.[24] The *Gazette* printed a total of 203 items on the revival from 1739 to 1748, only nineteen of which were negative. Ninety-four items were positive and ninety items were neutral. The *Boston Gazette* printed 125 news items, six of which were negative, and seventy-eight letters, thirteen of which were negative. In their two papers, the *New England Weekly Journal* and *Boston Gazette*, Kneeland and Green printed 307 items on the revival, 284 of which were positive or neutral. Coverage was consistent throughout the period 1739-1748. Reprints accounted for an average of approximately

32 percent of all items printed, while articles from the *Boston Gazette* and *Weekly Journal* were reprinted by other papers seventy-four times.

Boston also boasted the strongest opponent of the revival among its newspapermen. Printer Thomas Fleet, trained as a printer in England before arriving in the colonies in 1712, was by far the most resolute foe of the movement. Fleet assumed proprietorship of the paper *The Weekly Rehearsal* in April 1733, discontinuing it in August 1735. One week later, Fleet began printing a new paper titled *The Boston Evening-Post*. Fleet was known for displaying his wit in the *Post*, and often used it against supporters of the revival. Consider an example from the September 2, 1745, issue of the *Post* in which Fleet asks for subscribers in arrears to make their payments: "It is wonderful to observe, that while we hear so much said about a great Revival of Religion in the Land; there is yet so little Regard had to Justice and Common Honesty! Surely they are abominable good Works!"

Fleet's opposition to the revival and particularly to Whitefield was not apparent in the *Post*'s first few years of coverage of the movement. From 1739 until 1741, the *Post* printed forty-six items on the revival, with only twenty-five being negative. In 1742, however, the *Post* printed seventy-two items concerning the movement, fifty-seven of which were negative. In the next three years, the *Post* printed 145 negative items, three positive items, and twenty-four neutral items. For the years 1739-1748, the *Post* printed a total of 345 items on the Awakening, more by far than any other paper in the colonies except the *Boston Gazette*, almost 75 percent of which were negative.[25] Of the papers that reported significantly on the revival, the *Post* was one of the few that printed more letters than news items, with letters comprising almost 69 percent of Fleet's reporting.[26] Reprints constituted only 10 percent of items printed by the *Post*, by far the lowest percentage among papers with substantial coverage. Original reporting from the *Post* was reprinted by other papers seventy-six times.[27]

Because of their strong opinions on the Awakening, Fleet's *Boston Evening-Post* and Kneeland and Green's *Boston Gazette* frequently waged their own paper wars, with supporters of the revival using the *Gazette* to counter negative views expressed in the *Post*, and vice versa. This phenomenon made Boston the only colonial city in which "party papers" publicly argued over the Awakening. For example, on May 3,

1742, the *Post* published a news report on a dispute in the Rev. John Lowell's church in Newbury, Massachusetts. According to the *Post*, itinerant revivalists Nathaniel Rogers, Daniel Rogers, and Samuel Buell "took Possession" of Lowell's church while Lowell was away and proceeded to preach to the town's young people. They attempted to possess the Rev. Christopher Toppan's church the next day but were "repulsed." Fleet ended his report with this comment: "These Itinerants aim very much at dividing the Churches, and disaffecting People to their faithful Pastors, and what wild Scheme they are pursuing next, God only knows." On May 18, the *Gazette* countered with a letter from a contributor from Newbury named John Brown who attempted to clarify and defend the actions of the itinerants.[28] The next week, the May 24 issue of the *Post* responded with a letter from the Rev. Lowell himself, asserting the truth of Fleet's first report and claiming he had the depositions to prove it. John Brown responded again in the *Gazette* on June 29, and the *Post* printed a letter and certificate from Newbury contributor Henry Rolfe on July 5 in an effort to prove the improprieties committed by the revivalists. Boston is the only region with enough party papers to allow this type of back-and-forth arguing in multiple papers.

Boston reporting on Whitefield and his followers, besides being frequent and varied, was also influential, if one links influence to rate of reprinting. As noted above, Boston papers had the highest reprint percentage in the colonies when one counts reprints by region as percent of the whole. Of the 1598 items printed in newspapers during 1739 through 1748, 13 percent of those items were reprints from Boston papers. Philadelphia had the second-highest reprint percentage with 10 percent. Seventy-six items were reprinted from Fleet's *Evening Post* while seventy-four items were reprinted from Kneeland and Green's *New England Weekly Journal* and *Boston Gazette*. Only items from Benjamin Franklin's *Pennsylvania Gazette* were reprinted more often (88).

When one examines the most popular topics that New Englanders argued about in the newspapers in regard to religion in the 1740s, it is apparent that the most-discussed issues related to religious tradition and stability. Most of the arguments in the Boston papers pitted those who favored a traditional approach to religion that emphasized peace and order against those who advocated a more unconventional, emotional, sometimes disruptive spirituality, more in line with New Light thinking. One paper war from the summer of 1745 illustrates this tendency. In July 30, 1745, just after Whitefield had left Boston after a successful New England preaching tour, revival supporters used the *Boston Gazette* to call for a meeting to issue a statement of doctrine regarding the revival to help quell the divisions and separations the movement was spawning. The meeting, which occurred on September 25, produced *The Testimony of a Number of New-England Ministers Met at Boston Sept. 25. 1745* (Boston, 1745), and also provoked ten letters in Thomas Fleet's *Boston Evening-Post*.[29] A primary complaint of the majority of the *Post* letters was that the pro-revival clergymen were disturbing the spiritual "peace." One contributor on August 12 worried that the ministers were stirring up "fresh Controversies" just when "Harmony and Peace" had returned in the wake of Whitefield's departure. A layman whose letter appeared in the *Post* on October 21, 1745, reported that the ministers had indeed convened and wondered, "Whether these twenty five were Priests, or Princes of the Congregation, is uncertain; but certain it is, they were the Men, who by their mischievous Contrivances and wicked Counsels, greatly disturbed the public Peace, and emboldened Men in all manner of Impiety." The most original of the contributions, printed on August 26, suggested a particularly tangible response to the ministerial gathering:

> Mr. Fleet, I live upon the Banks of Merrimack, in a Place fertile in Birch Trees. . . . There are of all Sizes, fit for any Backsides you can imagine, from the most fat and plump, down to the most lean and skinny that will hardly bear a whipping; I send you this Notice, that, as I see there is like to be a great Demand for Birch towards the latter End of September next, you may know where to direct your Friend, for a Supply. Your's Timothy Wood.

Thus the primary topics discussed in the Boston paper wars flowed out of this fundamental disagreement over the value of maintaining the peace and order of the New England church community.

The first topic of discussion produced by this basic disagreement was the argument in Boston papers regarding itinerant preaching. Itinerant preaching was a topic of debate throughout the colonies in the mid-1740s, but it was discussed with special vehemence in Boston. After Whitefield left for England in January 1741, many clergymen who admired the evangelist began imitating his practice of itinerant preaching, traveling throughout the colonies, preaching in the open fields or to groups of listeners convened for that purpose. Even laymen, not ordained and sometimes unlearned, began preaching itinerantly, causing both Connecticut and New York to create laws forbidding the practice. Itinerant preaching was viewed by many as subversive to established ministers and churches and as dangerous to the spiritual climate of the colonies.[30] Proponents of the practice blamed established ministers for not providing the teaching their parishioners needed. During 1742, Boston experienced three paper wars over the practice of itinerancy.

Boston's first paper war over itinerant preaching was birthed in Newbury, Massachusetts, in the church of the Reverend John Lowell, as mentioned above, and involved five letters printed in the *Boston Evening-Post* and *Boston Gazette* from May to July of 1742.[31] A second paper war over itinerancy was carried on exclusively in the *Boston Weekly News-Letter*, published by John Draper. Five items appeared during the argument, beginning on October 28, 1742, and ending with the December 23 issue of the *News-Letter*. A portion of an anonymous letter which appeared in the November 25 issue of the *News-Letter* is perhaps the clearest representation of the anti-itinerancy view found in the Boston papers: "And certain and obvious it is, that the most, if not all of them are swell'd, and ready to burst with spiritual Pride. As to their Mission, they have none, except from their own fond Imagination. They indeed tell us of an immediate Call, and Assistances from Heaven. But can we believe them, while the Divisions and Disorders they create wherever they come, abundantly confute their Pretences. As to their Furniture for Preaching, the most of them are Babes in Knowledge; mere Novices in spiritual Things."

All of the Boston newspapers except the *Boston Weekly Post-Boy* participated in the third significant paper war over itinerancy. Spanning eight issues and running from November 1742 until January 1743, the argument appeared in the *Boston Gazette*, *Boston Evening-Post*, and *Boston Weekly News-Letter*. Five separate readers contributed letters to the debate and raised such topics as whether or not Jesus was an itinerant minster and if Congregational standards allowed for itinerancy.[32]

Debates over itinerant preaching dominated the Boston papers during the years following Whitefield's 1739-1741 preaching tour, ending for the most part by the summer of 1743. But itinerancy was not the only topic related to the spiritual tradition of the New England community that newspaper contributors debated during the 1740s. When Whitefield landed in York, Maine, in October 1744, for his second preaching tour of the colonies, conflict increased as it had during his first preaching tour. But, this time, the focus of discussion in the Boston papers was on the practice of discontented parishioners separating from established churches, which many saw as a direct consequence of itinerant preaching.[33] For example, on February 25, 1745, the *Boston Evening-Post* noted that Whitefield had preached twice at a Separate meeting in Newbury, Massachusetts, "notwithstanding his pretended Zeal against Separations." When the printers of the pro-Whitefield *Boston Gazette* failed to mention that Whitefield had preached at the meetings of separatists, the *Post* chided them on March 11.[34] *Gazette* printers Kneeland and Green did not reply publicly to this remark, but contented themselves with printing a report on Whitefield's latest preaching successes in their paper the next day.

One interesting contribution to the separatist debate appeared in the *Boston Evening-Post* on January 19, 1747. The contributor suggested that, instead of driving parishioners to form Separate congregations, the "Enthusiasm" of Whitefield had "given the most threatning [sic] Stroke of all to the Root of the Dissenting Interest in New-England" by driving many "sober and judicious" Congregationalists to the Church of England. The criticism sparked an argument between dissenters and Anglicans that produced six additional letters. Dissenters derided the Church of England for its "jewish and antichristian Pageantry," which included "the tinkling of Bells Psalterys and Organs, the garnishing a Church with Angels, Cherubims, Crosses &c. the ceremonious dressing of your Priests and your Services, with the observance of Days Months &c."[35] Anglicans countered with their list of revival excesses in the March 23 *Boston Evening-Post*: "Public Worship in the utmost Confusion, and endless Separations carrying on, and every thing going into Confusion, without Rule or Order, and indeed all Appearances of Rule and Order trampled upon by your Ministers themselves; together with the most wretched Nonsense of Extempore Effusions."

Besides itinerant preaching and church separations, another aspect of New England spiritual tradition that produced arguments in the Boston newspapers, particularly in Thomas Fleet's *Boston Evening-Post*, was the proper administration of the sacramental elements of the church, particularly baptism and ordination for ministry. On June 29, 1747, the *Boston Evening-Post* reported that revivalist ministers Nathanael Rogers and Daniel Rogers administered communion to separatists in Exeter, New Hampshire, and baptized some of their children. The ordinations of New Lights Daniel Rogers, Samuel Buell, and Joseph Adams were reported by the *Boston Evening-Post*, with the report on Buell revealing Fleet's disapproval most clearly: "We hear that the famous Mr. Bueul [sic] has lately been ordain'd a vagrant Preacher, by some Ministers in Connecticut." Fleet also reported on the ordinations of revivalist preachers Sylvanus Conant and Dudley Leavitt, which were conducted in apple orchards because they were refused churches: "'Tis remarkable, that here have been Two Orchard Ordinations within a few Months."[36]

Regardless of the topic under discussion, the public bickering that dominated Boston newspapers during the early 1740s had one final defining characteristic, one which perhaps most clearly set it apart from paper wars in other regions of the colonies. Specifically, the Boston paper wars were extremely personal and vituperative. The first two series of paper wars in Boston reveal this tendency. The first series was begun in the spring of 1742 by revivalist Andrew Croswell, a Congregational minister in Groton, Connecticut. An extreme proponent of the revival, Croswell traveled as an itinerant preacher, defended key revivalists such as Whitefield and James Davenport, and was a close friend of fellow itinerants Samuel Buell and Benjamin Pomeroy.[37]

The intensity of Croswell's support for the movement is revealed in the fact that in this first Boston paper war, Croswell did not hesitate to attack a moderate revivalist for what he considered to be Arminian sympathies.[38] On April 12, 1742, Croswell criticized fellow Boston clergyman Thomas Foxcroft for his preface to Jonathan Dickinson's *The True Scripture-Doctrine Concerning Some Important Points of Christian Faith* (Boston, 1741). Both Foxcroft and Dickinson were moderate supporters of the revival, thus making Croswell "rather prejudic'd in his [Foxcroft's] Favour," yet Croswell still accused

Foxcroft of being an Arminian: "It seemed good to me therefore, and for the Glory of my Master to expostulate with this Reverend Gentleman in a publick Manner; and since he will needs have Arminians to go to Heaven, to enquire of him, how will he get them there?"

Just a few months later, on July 5, 1742, the associated ministers of Boston and nearby Charlestown published a declaration against James Davenport that appeared in the *Boston Evening-Post*.[39] In response, Croswell published *Reply to the Declaration of a Number of the Associated Ministers in Boston and Charlestown* (Boston, 1742). On August 10, the pro-revival *Boston Gazette* printed an anonymous letter criticizing Croswell for his "furious Reply to the mild and gentle Declaration of the associated Ministers." Two weeks later, in the August 23 *Boston Weekly Post-Boy*, Croswell attacked the *Gazette* contributor for remaining anonymous, calling on readers to view the contributor's rebuke as a "cowardly Attack made by one of the Devil's Soldiers."

Fellow radical revivalist John Moorhead began the second paper war, which was even more acrimonious and replete with personal insults. A Presbyterian minister in Boston since 1730, Moorhead had immigrated to the colonies from Ireland at about the age of twenty-three and was considered unlearned, although he may have been ordained in Ireland.[40] Moorhead received much antipathy in the papers when he publicly questioned the authenticity of the ministerial qualifications of the Rev. John Caldwell of Londonderry, New Hampshire, opponent of the revival and author of the critique *An Impartial Trial of the Spirit Operating in this Part of the World* (Boston, 1742).[41] Contributors against Moorhead criticized his motives for writing and mercilessly attacked his supposed lack of learning.[42] In the December 27 *Boston Evening-Post*, an anonymous poet offered "On John M------d's stiling himself, The Rev'd John M------d":

> Ah, modest M------d, vain are all
> Thy Looks demure; in vain you join
> The Sacred Tribe, and fondly call
> Your self a Reverend Divine.
> So with some Apples, side by side,
> If honest Æsop tells us true,
> A Horse Turd floated down the Tide;
> And call'd it self an Apple too.

On January 3, 1743, *Boston Evening-Post* contributor A. W. remarked that Moorhead's letters revealed that although Moorhead supposedly "taught Greek and Latin in Ireland with Approbation, 'tis evident beyond Dispute, that he understands neither Sense nor English in New England." Z. H. commented in the same issue of the *Post* that he wished Moorhead's writings were "less obscure and perplex'd, for the sake of your Readers, who are generally observ'd to reap the most Advantage from Writings which they understand." The next week, Fleet printed the poem "Unlucky Jack. A Tale," which featured young Jack Moorhead throwing eggs at passersby and being "pummel'd for his Rogury." In the poem, Jack seeks protection from some men "dress'd like himself," yet when his defenders flee the blows of the crowd, Jack is left to "undergo due Punishment." The brutal sarcasm of these responses reveal the personal nature of many of the contributed letters in Boston.

Even the newspaper printers themselves attacked each other in Boston. For example, on December 3, 1744, Fleet reported in his *Boston Evening-Post* that Whitefield had arrived in Boston to preach, but that he and his wife had not attended any sermons except Whitefield's own. The next day, the *Gazette* attempted to set the record straight, noting that physicians had "forbidden" Whitefield to be out at night. Kneeland and Green expressed their disapproval of the *Post*'s "false and abusive Reflections in the Evening Post on that Gentlewoman [Mrs. Whitefield], as soon as she arrives an harmless Stranger among us," remarking that Mrs. Whitefield had in fact attended a lecture that was not preached by her husband. On December 10, Fleet apologized for his mistake regarding Mrs. Whitefield, but criticized Kneeland and Green for printing that Whitefield merely "assisted" with communion at Benjamin Colman's church when, in fact, Whitefield had actually administered the sacrament himself. The disagreement over communion continued in four more letters in the *Gazette* and *Post*.

By the time of Whitefield's second preaching tour in New England in 1744, however, supporters and opponents of the revival in Boston began to take divergent courses in how they utilized the newspapers. While opponents continued and even increased the vitriol in their attacks, usually using Thomas Fleet's *Boston Evening-Post* to do so, revival supporters stopped responding at all in the papers.

An example of this divergence is the attack on revival supporter Thomas Foxcroft in Fleet's *Post* in the late winter and early spring of 1745. Six contributed letters criticized Foxcroft's published defense of Whitefield, *An apology in behalf of the Revd. Mr. Whitefield* (Boston, 1745).[43] On February 11, 1745, Foxcroft was criticized for his decision to "THRUST" himself into the "present Controversy, in behalf of Mr. Whitefield," forsaking the "Peace" of his own church. In the same issue, another writer warned Foxcroft that he had entered a war zone: "As you have enter'd a Volunteer in the present Paper War, I doubt not you are prepar'd for all Encounters, and ready to act offensively or defensively as the Vicissitudes of the War may require. Nor may you dream of putting off the Harness in a short Time, since it is probable there will not be a speedy Discharge in this War." The most recognized contributor appeared on March 25, when Fleet devoted the entire first page of the *Post* to an excerpt of a letter from South Carolina Anglican Commissary Alexander Garden which called Foxcroft's work "the compleatest Piece, I think, of pure Wrangle that ever I set Eyes on." Garden chastened Foxcroft for "becoming a Tool for another."

No defenders of Foxcroft appeared in the extant newspapers, nor did any *Post* letter mention a response. Three years earlier, when Andrew Croswell criticized Foxcroft in April 1742 for his introduction to Dickinson's *True Scripture-Doctrine Concerning Some Important Points of Christian Faith*, three defenders and Foxcroft himself appeared in the papers to refute the attack. Apparently, Boston revival supporters had begun to question the efficacy of utilizing the newspapers to respond to personal attacks. Perhaps revivalists had seen that the venom of the controversies of the previous several years had not endeared the movement to many.

Frequent, varied, influential, personal, and, at times, brutally sarcastic—these characteristics describe the New England paper wars over the religious events of the early 1740s. The issues being debated revolved around the place of tradition in the spiritual community. Should itinerant preaching be allowed and itinerant ministers ordained? Are peace and order the most important qualities of a church? How far should a community stray from its spiritual roots? Questions like these were debated viciously in the Boston papers, making New England the most noteworthy region of the colonies for local paper wars.

MIDDLE COLONIES: PHILADELPHIA

The Middle Colonies of Pennsylvania, New York, Virginia, and Maryland had newspapers publishing during the events of the Awakening, although only Philadelphia and New York enjoyed multiple papers. Coverage of the Awakening in the Middle Colonies reveals most clearly the reality that differing factors could produce newspaper coverage that varied greatly.

In Pennsylvania and New Jersey, for example, some regions were almost as prepared for revival as was New England. For several decades before Whitefield's arrival, small revivals had occurred throughout New Jersey and Pennsylvania. These movements tended to follow the Scottish revivalist tradition in which the New Birth was a lengthy process accompanied by much soul-searching and religious instruction.[44] A pioneer in these revivals was Dutch Reformed minister Theodore Frelinghuysen, who had been preaching evangelistic, pietistic sermons to his New Brunswick, New Jersey, congregation since the early 1720s. Although his emphasis on the New Birth and a disciplined spiritual life sometimes caused conflict with other clergymen, Frelinghuysen brought revival to many lay people and produced many new converts.

Frelinghuysen also strongly influenced a family of preachers, the Tennents. William Tennent, Sr., had left the Anglican church and embraced Presbyterianism before leaving his native Ireland. Soon after starting his ministry in Neshaminy, Pennsylvania, in 1725, Tennent formed the Log College, an evangelical seminary that trained Presbyterian ministers and emphasized not only the traditional ministerial curriculum, but evangelism and experiential piety as well. Tennent's sons Gilbert, John, and William, Jr., all graduates of the Log College, pastored New Jersey Presbyterian congregations in New Brunswick, Hopewell, and Freehold, respectively, and followed Frelinghuysen's evangelical approach to ministry. The Tennents enjoyed revival in their congregations in the early 1730s.[45] Other evangelical preachers such as John Cross, Samuel Blair, and Eleazer Wales settled in the area and experienced small revivals of their own.[46] During the Awakening, these pastors played important roles in extending the revival throughout the Middle Colonies and in connecting that movement with the revival in New England.

In Philadelphia, the largest city in the area, the region's openness to revival and evangelical practice combined with several additional factors to influence how Philadelphia papers covered the religious events of the 1740s. First, Whitefield and other revivalists preached in the city often and had consistent support from revival-minded local pastors. Whitefield's popularity was perhaps greatest in Philadelphia when compared with other regions. Philadelphia also enjoyed a more diverse population and more religious tolerance and diversity than that found in Boston.[47] These factors led to a more open, accepting approach by the Philadelphia papers when covering the revival as compared to the more critical attitude of many of the Boston newspapers. In addition, the presence of Benjamin Franklin in the city ensured that Whitefield and his followers would receive steady coverage as Franklin was the principal colonial printer of Whitefield's works and a personal friend of the evangelist. Franklin printed his first story on Whitefield in the December 22, 1737, issue of the *Pennsylvania Gazette*, noting the evangelist's plan to visit the new colony of Georgia on a charity mission. Franklin continued to report on Whitefield in his *Gazette* and, when the evangelist arrived in Philadelphia in November 1739, Franklin contracted with Whitefield to print copies of his journals and sermons. Franklin later estimated that printing the evangelist's writings tripled the number of titles he produced. Before Whitefield, Franklin had devoted less than 5 percent of the *Gazette*'s editorial space to religion.[48]

The two men were also lifelong friends, with Whitefield sometimes staying with Franklin when the evangelist visited Philadelphia. As a youth in Boston, Franklin had satirized Puritan Christianity, and later in life did not appear to deviate much from his early views, despite learning discretion in sharing them.[49] In Philadelphia, he made financial contributions to the church his wife Deborah attended, the Anglican Christ Church in Philadelphia, although he seldom attended himself.[50] Apparently, Franklin and Whitefield's differing religious sentiments were not an obstacle; as Franklin notes in his autobiography: "[W]e had no religious Connection. He us'd indeed sometimes to pray for my Conversion, but never had the Satisfaction of believing that his Prayers were heard. Ours was a mere civil Friendship, sincere on both Sides, and lasted to his Death."[51] Scholars have suggested that Franklin was impressed with Whitefield's integrity, entrepreneurial spirit, and commitment to service, despite their differing religious views.[52]

The *Pennsylvania Gazette* printed some of the most glowing endorsements of Whitefield that appeared in colonial newspapers, most of which were written by Franklin. On October 23, 1740, the *Gazette* reported on Whitefield's farewell sermon to 20,000 listeners in Philadelphia and included this assessment of his ministry:

> He has been in and about this Town for this three Weeks last past: In all he has preach'd Forty-eight Times in Publick, besides expounding and exhorting in private. Vast Bodies of People have crowded every where to hear him; and great and remarkable, and we hope saving Impressions have been on great Numbers. Upward of Five Hundred Pounds Sterling in publick Contributions and private Benefactions have been collected for the Orphan-House in Georgia; great Additions would in all Probability be made to it, could he stay longer amongst us.

Interestingly, while revival supporters such as Boston printers Kneeland and Green supported the movement as a whole in their papers, Franklin focused the majority of his support on Whitefield, in whom he had a significant publishing interest.

Andrew Bradford, the son of New York printer William Bradford, began publishing his *American Weekly Mercury* in Philadelphia in 1719, and also offered strong coverage of the Awakening, but only in the early years. During 1739, the *Mercury* printed twenty-two items; this number almost doubled the next year when forty items appeared in the paper. Coverage was overwhelmingly positive or neutral in those years. Only ten items were printed in 1741, but that number doubled the next year with twenty-one items appearing, many of which followed the national trend toward more negative reporting on the movement. After 1742, Bradford's coverage of revival events decreased. Andrew Bradford's nephew and foster son, William Bradford, Jr., began the city's third weekly newspaper, the *Pennsylvania Journal*, on December 2, 1742, and he followed Whitefield's 1744-1748 preaching tour carefully, printing over half of the *Journal*'s seventy-six total items on the revival during 1746 and 1747, when controversy surrounding the evangelist was strong.

Philadelphia coverage of the revival had some similarities to reporting in Boston, but some differences as well. In terms of amount of coverage, newspaper reporting on the revival in Philadelphia was like that of Boston. In fact, Philadelphia papers were second to Boston papers in the amount of coverage provided of Whitefield and the revival. Philadelphia's total of 376 items was less than half the number of items printed by Boston papers, but more than the amount of items printed by newspapers in all other parts of the colonies combined. The number and tone of revival-related newspaper items printed in Philadelphia is shown in Figure 2.4.

Andrew Bradford's *American Weekly Mercury* printed 136 items on the revival during the years 1739-1748, placing it behind only the *Boston Evening-Post* (345), *Boston Gazette* (203), *Pennsylvania Gazette* (164), and *South-Carolina Gazette* (149).[53] William Bradford, Jr.'s *Pennsylvania Journal* printed seventy-six items on the revival during the years 1742-1748. Benjamin Franklin's *Pennsylvania Gazette* covered Whitefield and the movement the most closely, printing a total of 164 items on the revival, with only the *Boston Evening-Post* and *Boston Gazette* printing more. In fact, the *Pennsylvania Gazette* was the most reprinted newspaper on the Awakening, with items from the *Gazette* appearing in other papers eighty-eight times.

Yet, reporting on the revival in Philadelphia, while similar in amount, was very different from reporting in Boston in terms of content and tone. Whitefield and the revival were supported strongly in Philadelphia, without the intense level of opposition found in the Boston papers. While positive or neutral items made up slightly less than 60 percent of the coverage in Boston papers, almost 80 percent of the items in Philadelphia papers were either positive or neutral toward the Awakening. Andrew Bradford's *American Weekly Mercury* printed eighty-five positive or neutral items on the revival, while fifty-one items were negative. All but two of the revival-related items printed in William Bradford, Jr.'s *Pennsylvania Journal* were positive or neutral, and only approximately 15 percent of all items in Franklin's *Pennsylvania Gazette* were negative toward the revival.

Philadelphia papers also focused more strongly on updating their readers on news of the revival and Whitefield, not debating, as was the case in Boston. While letters constituted more than 50 percent of printed items in Boston, only slightly more than 35 percent of all items printed in Philadelphia papers were letters. The *American Weekly Mercury*'s coverage was evenly split between letters and news reports, but the *Pennsylvania Journal* offered only fourteen letters out of sixty-two total items. Among the total number of revival-related items printed in the *Pennsylvania Gazette*, only slightly more than 30 percent were letters, revealing that Philadelphia readers received more news on the movement and less debate than did Boston readers.

Yet, Philadelphians did debate aspects of the Awakening, and the topics they chose to discuss were quite different from those of Boston. While Bostonians primarily debated issues concerning religious tradition such as the appropriateness of itinerant preaching, church separations, and the unauthorized performance of the Christian sacraments, Philadelphians discussed topics that often revolved around the question of authenticity. Whitefield's honesty as a minister of the gospel, the accuracy of newspaper accounts on the Awakening, the genuineness of emotionalist preaching—these were some of the matters that Philadelphians debated in the papers. As such, readers of these papers expressed less concern for the influence of New Light teaching and practice on the church as an institution and more for its truthfulness as a movement.

George Whitefield's authenticity as a clergyman was at the center of several paper wars in Philadelphia. His financial integrity was often questioned, as Whitefield received large amounts of donated funds during his preaching tours. Whitefield's only direct refutation of financial attacks in a colonial newspaper appeared in the *Pennsylvania Gazette* on May 22, 1746, in which Whitefield published his financial accounts for his orphanage in Savannah, Georgia.[54] On April 23, 1747, the *Pennsylvania Gazette* reprinted a report from the *South-Carolina Gazette* on Whitefield's receipt of monetary donations from the town of Charleston for his use "as he thinks fit." Franklin added the following comment to his reprinting of the report: "The above Extracts will, we doubt not, at once please the Friends of the Reverend Mr. Whitefield, and convince every candid Reader, that his Accounts of the Disposition of the Sums of Money heretofore collected for the Use of his Orphan House in Georgia are just; since it cannot be conceived that Gentlemen, who live so near to that House as Charles-Town, South-Carolina, and have daily Opportunities of knowing how the Affair is conducted, should contribute so generously to Mr. Whitefield, if they thought his former Collections were not duly applied."

Whitefield's political loyalties were also questioned by the public, particularly during England's troubles with Spain in the 1740s. On August 28, 1746, Franklin lauded Whitefield's loyalty to the Crown as well as his superior preaching: "Last Sunday Evening the Rev. Mr. Whitefield preach'd to a very large Auditory (among whom were many of the principal Persons of this City) a most excellent Sermon on Occasion of the late Victory over the Rebels [in the Jacobite Rebellion of 1745-1746]. . . . No Discourse of his among us has given more general Satisfaction; nor has the Preacher ever met with a more universal Applause; having demonstrated himself to be as sound and zealous a Protestant, and as truly a loyal Subject, as he is a grand and masterly Orator." Franklin affirmed Whitefield's loyalty to the king of England to quiet some critics who were alleging that Whitefield was working as an agent of the queen of Spain.

Readers in Philadelphia also focused strongly on the accuracy of written reports regarding Whitefield and other aspects of the revival. In Philadelphia, the papers showed a consistent effort to properly estimate the number of listeners at revivalist messages. For example, the *American Weekly Mercury* reported on May 22, 1740, that Whitefield had preached a farewell sermon before he left Philadelphia to "near 20,000 hearers." When the evangelist preached another farewell sermon in Philadelphia in the fall of 1740, the *Mercury* reported that "some say" the number of listeners was 30,000, but it was "generally computed" to be 25,000. A news item from the *Mercury* for December 6, 1739, provides an example of specificity in reporting: "On Thursday last the Rev. Mr. Whitefield left this City [Philadelphia], and was accompany'd as far as Chester by about 150 Horse where he Preach'd to about 5000 People; on Friday he preach'd twice at Willings Town to about 5000; on Saturday at New Castle to about 2000, and the same Evening at Christiana Bridge to about 3000; on Sunday at Whiteclay Creek he Preached twice, resting about half an hour between the Sermons, to about 8000, of whom about 3000 'tis computed came on Horse-back." In his autobiography, *Pennsylvania Gazette* printer Benjamin Franklin recalled the method he used to arrive at the conclusion that Whitefield could be heard by "more than Thirty-Thousand."[55] Still, some Philadelphia readers questioned the truthfulness of the reports on Whitefield's preaching. One contributor to the *Pennsylvania Gazette* on May 8, 1740, complained that the number of attendees at Whitefield's preaching stops was "always exaggerated, being often doubled or trebled."

A similar battle over precise wording occurred in the Philadelphia papers in the spring of 1743. At that time, concern was growing among revivalists about the orthodoxy and popularity of the Moravian sect. Although many Moravians were strong supporters of the revival, not all revivalists believed them to be orthodox in their beliefs, producing arguments in the revival camp.[56] Gilbert Tennent had been preaching against the Moravians since 1742 and in 1743 published *The Necessity of Holding Fast the Truth* (Boston), to which was appendixed *Some Account of the Principles of the Moravians*, in an attempt to discredit the movement. On April 7, 1743, Moravian bishop Peter Boehler of the Moravian congregation in Bethlehem, Pennsylvania, advertised in the *Pennsylvania Gazette* that all translations of Moravian writings done by members of his congregation would henceforth carry his signature to ensure their authenticity. Boehler complained that "sundry Persons" had translated Moravian writings from the German incorrectly, causing the Moravian brethren to be "misrepresented and misunderstood." On April 14, a contributor to the *American Weekly Mercury* attacked Boehler for his "Presumption" in dictating to readers which translations of Moravian writings were acceptable, as if he could "restrain not only the Press but the Publick from their legal and national Rights." Excerpts of Moravian leader Count Zinzendorf's correspondence were printed in both the original German and an English translation by Joseph Crellius, so that "the Publick may reasonably guess at their [the Moravians'] Principles, and take Caution thereby." Both the *Pennsylvania Gazette* and *Mercury* items were reprinted by the April 25 *New-York Weekly Post-Boy*, while the April 25 *New-York Weekly Journal* reprinted the *Mercury* piece. Although this quarrel was short-lived, it was one more skirmish over authenticity in the movement. Because of the revival's importance as a news event, both revivalists and their opponents relied heavily on all forms of written media to spread their messages, and readers wanted to ensure they had access to accurate writings by both sides.

The authenticity of the revival experience also concerned Philadelphia readers, as one paper war in the summer of 1740 reveals. Presbyterian evangelist John Rowland joined with other New Lights to preach in Presbyterian and Baptist churches during the summer session of the Philadelphia Presbyterian Synod. Rowland delivered a hellfire-and-brimstone diatribe to the Philadelphia Baptist Church on Thursday evening, July 3, 1740. Three days later, with Philadelphia Baptist senior pastor Jenkin Jones away, associate pastor Ebenezer Kinnersley used his morning sermon to proclaim his disapproval of Rowland's preaching methods. Kinnersley's complaints focused on the dubious methods used by Rowland to stir up false emotions, or a false experience, in his listeners: "Such whining, roaring Harangues, big with affected Nonsense, have no other Tendency, but to operate upon the softer Passions, and work them up to a warm Pitch of Enthusiasm, which when the Preacher has done, he has fully gain'd his End, and goes away rejoicing in his triumphant Conquests over weak Minds." Kinnersley asserted that the results of emotional preaching were "very notorious" in Philadelphia, causing some listeners to be "terrified to Distraction; others drove into Dispair [sic]; others wishing themselves in the same condition . . . while others are fill'd brim-full of Enthusiastic Raptures and Extasies."[57] Many in the church disagreed with Kinnersley's assessment of Rowland, and on Saturday, July 12, Kinnersley was found guilty at a church meeting of opposing Rowland's preaching. He was barred from attending church the next day.

Kinnersley's attack on revivalist preaching focused on the experience of parishioners while listening to such sermons. To Kinnersley, what listeners experienced was not authentic, biblical Christianity, but, instead, an emotional roller coaster in which the passions were stimulated but the spirit remained untouched. On Tuesday, July 15, Kinnersley wrote a defense of himself, which contained an excerpt of his offending sermon and some criticisms of Jones and members of the Baptist church. Franklin printed the letter in the postscript to the July 24 *Pennsylvania Gazette*, noting that although he did not approve of printing "Invectives," he printed Kinnersley's letter to allow the minister to defend himself and to quell criticism that he and other Philadelphia printers showed "great Partiality in favour of the [revivalist] Preaching lately admir'd among us." Kinnersley's letter again reveals a preoccupation with dishonesty and legitimacy. In his letter, Kinnersley condemned the church group that had found him guilty, claiming the entire episode manifested a "Spirit of Lying." He repeated his criticism that Rowland's preaching was "designing, artful and deluding," enabling Rowland to "reign Tyrant over the Passions" of the congregation. Kinnersley rejected his congregation's request that he make what he termed a "hypocritical Confession," and he blamed the Rev. Jones for "artful Evasion" and for "telling Untruths" to both God and the people. He claimed he had offered *Gazette* readers a "true Account of this Affair."

In August, nine men of the congregation of the Philadelphia Baptist Church met with Kinnersley and discussed the matter. Seven of the nine judged Kinnersley "worthy of Reproof" and placed an advertisement in the August 14 *Pennsylvania Gazette* defending both Jones against Kinnersley's charges of "speaking Untruths" as well as the committee against charges of irregular proceedings. Although the committee claimed in their advertisement that they were unwilling to "render Railing for Railing," the dispute continued in pamphlets for several months.[58] Kinnersley's battle with the Philadelphia Baptist Church was one more instance of Philadelphia readers' interest in evaluating the genuineness of the revival movement.

MIDDLE COLONIES: NEW YORK

Newspaper coverage of the Awakening in New York reveals how varied reporting on the movement was in the Middle Colonies. Although close to Philadelphia geographically, New York readers had a significantly different experience of the revival through the newspapers. Three characteristics emerge of the coverage of the Awakening in the New York newspapers—limited, neutral, and derivative.

Two weekly newspapers were publishing in New York at the time of Whitefield's arrival in the colonies in 1739, and those papers combined to print only thirty-eight items on the revival during Whitefield's first colonial preaching tour (October 1739-January 1741). By the beginning of Whitefield's second tour in 1744, two additional papers had begun in New York. Still, even with four newspapers, New York readers enjoyed only fifty-seven articles on the revival during White-field's second tour. In total, during the years 1739 through 1748, New York papers printed 157 items on the Awakening—much less than the 885 items printed by Boston papers or the 376 items printed by the papers in Philadelphia. Of the 157 items printed in New York papers on the revival, fifty were positive, thirty-seven negative, and seventy neutral, as shown in Figure 2.5. Thus, almost one-half of New York reporting on the revival was neutral.

Some factors can account for New York's limited and neutral cover-age of the revival. New York did not have a revival heritage like that of New England and the Philadelphia/New Jersey area, and Whitefield drew much smaller crowds in New York City than he did in Boston and Philadelphia.[59] Upon Whitefield's arrival in New York City in November 1739, he visited the Anglican commissary of New York, William Vesey, and recorded a less than hospitable welcome: "Waited upon Mr. Vessey [sic]; but wished, for his own sake, he had behaved in a more Christian manner. He seemed to be full of anger and resent-ment, and before I asked him for the use of his pulpit, denied it" (348). Whitefield also noted in his journal the lack of revival tradition in New York: "I find that little of the work of God has been seen in [New York] for many years" (349).

Another factor that may have influenced New York reporting on the Awakening was a legal battle that occurred five years before White-field's first preaching visit to the colonies. Rival political factions in New York had instigated a continuing print war between the two New York newspapers then in existence. Supporters of New York governor William Cosby used William Bradford's *New-York Gazette* to dis-seminate their viewpoints, while the anti-Cosby faction had induced a young printer named John Peter Zenger to begin the *New-York Weekly Journal* in 1733 to advocate their perspective. On November 17, 1734, Zenger was arrested and imprisoned for seditious libel. During his imprisonment, which lasted almost one year, Zenger continued to pub-lish his *Weekly Journal* and Bradford continued to battle Zenger with his *Gazette*. Philadelphia attorney Andrew Hamilton was called in to defend Zenger, and on August 4, 1735, Zenger's trial began. Attorney General Richard Bradley focused his case upon proving that Zenger had indeed published the libelous material. Instead of attempting to deny that fact, Hamilton admitted it and asked the jury to determine whether the assertions in Zenger's paper were true or not. Hamilton argued that if the material in question was true, it was not libelous. Zenger was acquitted and returned to printing his *Weekly Journal*.[60]

The fact that printers Bradford and Zenger had experienced legal and public conflict for several years before the Awakening commenced may account somewhat for their lackluster approach to covering Whitefield and the revival during the early years of the movement. Whitefield was a controversial figure even before he landed in the colonies in the fall of 1739, and perhaps Bradford and Zenger were not enthusiastic about becoming embroiled in fresh paper wars. Unfortunately for Bradford, as noted in the introduction to this book, he became entangled in the first colonial paper war over Whitefield and the Awakening, printing on November 17, 1739, a pamphlet titled "To the Inhabitants of New-York," in which New York clergyman Jonathan Arnold criticized Whitefield. Published only eighteen days after Whitefield arrived in the colonies, Arnold's pamphlet enraged readers, and Arnold was attacked in newspapers in Philadelphia and Boston. He defended himself in the first two pages of Bradford's *Gazette* on January 22, 1740. Also in the January 22 *Gazette* was a letter which ran one and one-half pages defending Whitefield.

A comment inserted by Bradford between the two letters may provide insight into Bradford's reaction to the contention:

> The Publishers of this Gazette, hereby inform their Readers, That it was by strong Importunity they were induced to give the fore-going Letter [Arnold's] a Place herein. And since we have done it, we could not avoid inserting this which follows, without displeasing several of our constant Readers, whom we have refused, for several Weeks past, to Print it in our Paper. But upon their hearing, that we had agreed to Print Mr. Arnolds [sic] Letter, we could not (upon their reiterated Requests) refuse. And we hereby give Notice, that for the future we do not think to incert [sic] any more of these Controversies, not being proper for this Paper.

Bradford printed only seven more items on the revival that year in his *Gazette*, none of them controversial. The items were mostly updates on Whitefield's travels through the colonies or letters supportive of the revival and Whitefield. Arnold's letter of January 22 was the only negative item Bradford printed on the movement during 1739 and 1740. Few copies of the *Gazette* are extant for the years 1741-1744, so it is impossible to determine how closely Bradford covered the revival during those years, but reprints of revival-related articles from the *New-York Gazette* do not appear in other newspapers. Zenger printed more revival-related items in his *Weekly Journal* than did any other New York newspaper printer, but of his sixty-four items, thirty-nine were either positive or neutral.

The derivative nature of New York reporting on the Awakening is seen in the reprint percentage for the colony. Overall, during the years 1739 through 1748, 54 percent of all revival-related items appearing in New York papers were reprints from other newspapers. Only 3 percent of all items printed in the colonies on the Awakening during those years were reprinted items from New York newspapers. Sixty-three letters regarding the movement appeared in the New York papers, about one-third of which were negative, and ninety-four news reports were printed, the majority of which were neutral. Reprints accounted for 55 percent of Zenger's articles on the revival and 46 percent of Bradford's printing on the movement. Bradford discontinued his *New-York Gazette* sometime in November 1744 and turned the business over to his former apprentice and partner Henry DeForeest. DeForeest began the *New-York Evening-Post*, and one-third of DeForeest's revival items were reprints.

The fourth paper to begin during this time in New York is an exception in that its coverage of the religious events of the time was neither neutral nor derivative and reveals again the varying influence on how printers covered the Awakening. New Jersey native James Parker began his own printing business in the city in 1742 through a partnership with Benjamin Franklin.[61] On January 3, 1743, Parker established the *New-York Weekly Post-Boy*, which ran until January 12, 1747, when it became the *New-York Gazette, Revived in the Weekly Post-Boy*, without a change in numbering.[62] Unlike the other New York printers, Parker followed the revival closely in his paper, printing a total of fifty-five revival-related items for the years 1743-1748, inclusive. Although 60 percent of these items were reprints, items from Parker's paper were reprinted eighteen times, more than any other New York paper. Forty-one of Parker's items were news reports, giving his paper even more extensive news coverage of the revival than John Peter Zenger's *New-York Weekly Journal* offered. Parker printed only eight negative items, constituting less than 15 percent of all revival items published in his paper. His coverage of the revival was strongest during 1745 and 1746, when Whitefield was in the colonies for his second preaching tour. Parker's strong, supportive coverage is not surprising because of his connection with Franklin in Philadelphia, Whitefield's official colonial printer. That connection was perhaps the reason Parker's coverage of the Awakening differed significantly from that of his New York colleagues.

MARYLAND AND VIRGINIA

The more agrarian Chesapeake colonies of Maryland and Virginia each had one weekly newspaper printing during the time of the Awakening, and newspaper coverage of the movement in those colonies reveals again the influence of individual printers.[63] Neither colony boasted a strong revival tradition. The Rev. Thomas Bacon, a writer and clergyman of colonial Maryland, noted that deism was widespread throughout the colony.[64] Whitefield preached in several areas of Maryland during his first preaching tour. Upon arriving in the northeastern region of Maryland in early December 1739, Whitefield noted in his journal that Maryland was "a place yet unwatered with the true Gospel of Christ, and with no likelihood of much good being done in it," although perhaps soon God would "visit these dark corners of the earth" (365). Whitefield preached to "small polite auditories" in Annapolis and complained that the city suffered from "a false politeness, and the pomps and vanities of the world, eat out the vitals of religion in this place" (368).

The only newspaper printer in Maryland was Jonas Green, who began the *Maryland Gazette* on January 17, 1745.[65] A member of the well-known printing dynasty of Boston and brother of *Boston Gazette* printer Timothy Green, Jr., Green worked for Andrew Bradford in Philadelphia until he moved to Annapolis to serve as the colony's printer.

Green included much local literature in his *Gazette* and was a long-standing member of Alexander Hamilton's Tuesday Club, a popular and important social club founded in Annapolis by Hamilton in 1745 in which gentlemen met and discussed topics of interest.[66] Although we do not have Green's personal comments on Whitefield or the Awakening, we do have Hamilton's views on Whitefield from his record of club proceedings. In his *History of the Ancient and Honorable Tuesday Club*, Hamilton criticizes Whitefield for "giving them [his followers] first a Glimmering of the road or path, and then leaving them as much in the dark as ever."[67] Hamilton also criticizes the "stark nonsense" of Whitefield and the New Light preachers, who, although they have nothing to offer in what they say, "yet never fail to surprise and move their hearers, by the strength of their action, and bodily gesture alone."[68] As the "Poet Laureate and Master of Ceremonies" of the Tuesday Club, Jonas Green certainly may have agreed with Hamilton's assessment of Whitefield and the revival.

Whatever his personal view on the movement, Green did not cover the revival closely in his *Maryland Gazette*. For example, Whitefield visited Maryland several times on his second preaching tour of the colonies, but only once did the *Gazette* note his visit (November 11, 1746). When Whitefield preached before the Council and Assembly in Annapolis, Green's *Gazette*, printing since January 1745, did not report the stop, although Benjamin Franklin's *Pennsylvania Gazette* did (October 10, 1745). The total number of revival-related items printed by the *Gazette* for the years encompassing Whitefield's second colonial preaching tour stands at seven items, four of which were news items and three of which were letters. No items were clearly positive regarding the Awakening, three items were neutral, and four items were negative. Only one item was a reprint. The limited coverage of the Awakening by Green's *Maryland Gazette* can perhaps be attributed to the absence of both a revival history in the colony and a personal interest from the printer.

In Virginia, the Anglican church was the established church of the colony and had a strong presence in eastern Virginia, while the Scotch-Irish and German immigrants of western Virginia practiced a Reformed, pietistic faith more in line with New Light beliefs.[69] Like Maryland, Virginia did not have a strong revival tradition. However, Virginia printer William Parks appears to have had more of a personal interest in covering the revival. Parks, founder of the original *Maryland*

Gazette in 1727, established the *Virginia Gazette* in August 1736, having moved his residence from Maryland to Williamsburg, Virginia, in 1730. Parks received advice from Benjamin Franklin in setting up his print shops and is considered by many to be the most influential colonial printer after Franklin because of his encouragement of belletristic literature in the South and his entrepreneurial spirit. Parks was a nominal Anglican, serving as a vestryman of Bruton Church in Virginia, but, in actuality, he may have been more of a deist.[70]

Perhaps Parks' connection with Franklin was the source of his more concerted coverage of the Awakening because Parks' *Virginia Gazette* followed Whitefield even before he arrived in the colonies, as did Franklin's *Pennsylvania Gazette*, printing a report on the evangelist as early as January 1738. Before Whitefield's December 1739 visit to Williamsburg, the *Virginia Gazette* printed fourteen news items on Whitefield and the revival, reprinting reports of Whitefield's travels from both English and colonial newspapers. When Whitefield preached in Williamsburg in December 1739, the *Virginia Gazette* printed a positive report of his visit on December 21, noting his "extraordinary Manner of Preaching, gains him the Admiration and Applause of most of his Hearers." It appears from the *Gazette*'s coverage of Whitefield and the Awakening for 1739 that Parks' intention was to keep his readers aware of the progress of the movement throughout the colonies.

Unfortunately, although revival activity increased greatly in Virginia during the early 1740s, very few copies of the *Virginia Gazette* are extant for the years 1740 through 1744, so it is impossible to determine how closely the *Gazette* followed the movement. Of the five revival-related items printed in the issues that are extant for 1740, all of them were reprints from newspapers in Boston, Philadelphia, and New York, revealing Parks' willingness to report on revival events in all parts of the colonies. Although the numbers are small, three-quarters of the *Gazette*'s twenty-four items on the movement from the years 1739 through 1748 were neutral or positive. Only four of the items were letters, and two of those letters were reprints. The two original letters printed in the *Gazette* both appeared on October 31, 1745, after Whitefield preached in Williamsburg; one was a positive report on Whitefield and his preaching, and one was a negative response to Whitefield. Perhaps like his mentor Franklin, Parks was willing to

report on persons and events that he believed appealed to his readership. The reporting on the Awakening by the *Maryland Gazette* and
Virginia Gazette reveal the influence a printer could have on the coverage of an event when newspapers were limited in a colony.

SOUTH CAROLINA

At the southern tip of the colonies, South Carolina was a religiously
mixed colony. Estimates place Anglicans as the largest denomination
with approximately 45 percent of the population, but the remaining
dissenting denominations were also strong.[71] Thomas Whitmarsh
began the *South-Carolina Gazette* on January 8, 1732. After Whitmarsh's death in 1733, Lewis Timothy printed the paper. The son of
Huguenot parents, Timothy, his wife Elizabeth, and their four children
had immigrated to Philadelphia in 1731, where Timothy joined Benjamin Franklin as a journeyman printer. Timothy also served as the
first librarian of the Library Company of Philadelphia. In November
1733, Franklin sponsored Timothy as his partner in a printing business
in Charleston, South Carolina. Franklin would supply the equipment
and receive one-third of the profits, while Timothy would run the business to earn his share. Timothy did well in Charleston, printing the
laws of the colony, becoming postmaster, and founding a benevolent
organization with other Huguenots. Unfortunately, his work in South
Carolina was short-lived, as he died in an accident in December 1738,
leaving six children and a pregnant wife. Elizabeth used her above-
average education and business sense to continue the *South-Carolina
Gazette*, becoming the first female newspaper editor in the colonies.
Franklin was impressed with her business sense, noting in his autobiography her success and attention to detail.[72] The eldest child, Peter
Timothy, assumed the business officially in 1746 and became well-
respected in the colony.[73]

Coverage of the religious events of the 1740s by the *South-Carolina
Gazette* reveals several characteristics of reporting on the Awakening
in the South. First, both Elizabeth and Peter Timothy covered the revival closely. The *Gazette* holds the distinction of printing the fourth-
highest number of revival-related items in the colonies during the years

1739-1748 with 149 items, behind only the *Boston Evening-Post*, *Boston Gazette*, and *Pennsylvania Gazette*. In fact, during 1740 and 1741, the *Gazette* printed more items on the revival than did any other newspaper in the colonies except the *New England Weekly Journal*. This is perhaps not surprising, since the Timothys' professional relationship with Benjamin Franklin gave them a strong connection to Whitefield's primary publisher in the North. In addition, much original reporting appeared in the *Gazette* with only 23 percent of the paper's reporting on the revival being reprints. Only the *Boston Evening-Post* (10 percent) and the *Boston Gazette* (22 percent) had lower reprint percentages.[74] Both sides received fair treatment in the *Gazette* as well. Approximately 40 percent of the total revival-related items in the paper were negative. However, during the contentious years of 1742 through 1746, the number of negative items in the *Gazette* matched or outnumbered positive and neutral items combined, which was similar to most other newspapers during those years. Coverage was also consistent throughout the years of Whitefield's first two preaching tours, 1739-1748.

A second and somewhat unique characteristic of the *South-Carolina Gazette*'s coverage of the Awakening is that even local controversies were intercolonial in their appeal. Certainly, the location of the *Gazette* as the only newspaper in the deep South and the paper closest to Whitefield's Savannah, Georgia, orphanage helped ensure this interest. Items printed in the *Gazette* were reprinted fifty-one times by other papers, making it the fourth most reprinted paper in the colonies.[75] Two legal controversies that arose in South Carolina during Whitefield's first preaching tour reveal the intercolonial appeal of the *Gazette*'s reporting. The first difficulty was ecclesiastical in nature and transpired in the summer of 1740 during Whitefield's second preaching stop in Charleston. Whitefield's refusal to use the Anglican Prayer Book in his services caused South Carolina Anglican Commissary Alexander Garden to call the evangelist to appear before an ecclesiastical court in Charleston on July 15, 1740. On July 18, the *South-Carolina Gazette* carried the story of Whitefield's appearance at a trial to "answer to Articles of Impeachment." The report was reprinted in both Philadelphia and New York—the *Pennsylvania Gazette* reprinted part of the report on August 21, the *New-York Weekly Journal* on August 25. During the trial, Whitefield appealed to the Lords Commissioners in England, effectively ending the proceedings in Charleston, but requiring that he prosecute his case within a period of one year, which he did not do. Thus, the Charleston court suspended Whitefield.[76] The *South-Carolina Gazette* noted the suspension on February 13, 1742, and the *Boston Weekly Post-Boy* reprinted the story on March 15.[77]

Whitefield preached through the rest of the colonies during the fall and early winter of 1740, returning south briefly before sailing for England on January 16, 1741. Despite his short stay in Charleston, Whitefield managed to run afoul of the authorities again, but this time the issue involved the secular government. Whitefield corrected for the press a letter from South Carolina planter Hugh Bryan. Printed by the *South-Carolina Gazette* on January 8, 1741, the letter proclaimed that a November 1740 fire in Charleston had been sent by God as his "just Judgments" against the city for its "Iniquities, and the Iniquities of our Province and Nation." On January 15, the *Gazette* printed a follow-up story of Whitefield's arrest for "being concern'd in correcting" Bryan's letter. Although no colonial newspaper reprinted Bryan's original letter, the report of Whitefield's arrest was reprinted by the *New-York Weekly Journal* (March 2), *Pennsylvania Gazette* (March 26), *New England Weekly Journal* (April 7), *Boston Weekly News-Letter* (April 9), and *Boston Evening-Post* (April 13).[78] The story even traveled across the Atlantic. On June 9, 1741, the *New England Weekly Journal* reprinted this notice from a London newspaper: "In a few Days will be publish'd an Account of his [Whitefield's] Trial before Commissary Garden; and also a Letter written by Mr. Hugh Bryan, for correcting which Mr. Whitefield was bound over to appear by his Attorney as this Day, at Charlestown in South Carolina." Discussion of the event occurred even in newspapers outside of Charleston. On May 5, the *New England Weekly Journal* printed a letter from a Charleston merchant to a recipient in Boston which linked the November fire to the town's "unchristian Persecution begun against the Rev. Mr. Whitefield" and other revivalists in the area.

The grand jury of South Carolina eventually brought Bryan up on charges, but Bryan wrote a letter of recantation and apology to William Bull, Speaker of the Commons,[79] in which Bryan confessed to having fallen "into a Delusion of Satan" in his recent religious prophecies. The *South-Carolina Gazette* printed Bryan's apology on March 6,

1742, and the apology was reprinted by the *Boston Weekly Post-Boy* (May 3) and the *American Weekly Mercury* in Philadelphia (June 24). The May 3 *Post-Boy* also included an extract from a letter from South Carolina reporting on the recantation of Bryan. One year later, the *Boston Evening-Post* printed an excerpt from a letter from South Carolina which claimed that "Enthusiasm" in the colony had subsided since the "famous Hugh Briant [sic], sousing himself into the River Jordan, in order to smite and divide its Waters, had his Eyes opened." The *Post* report was reprinted by the *American Weekly Mercury* on May 19 and the *New-York Weekly Journal* on June 6. This amount of reprinting related to a local controversy is unique among colonial newspaper coverage of the Awakening.

The paper wars in the *South-Carolina Gazette* are also noteworthy for being lengthy with numerous contributors. For example, the first paper war in the *Gazette* began one week after Whitefield's first appearance in Charleston during his first colonial preaching tour. Whitefield preached several times in Charleston after arriving on January 5, 1740, and on January 12, the *South-Carolina Gazette* printed a letter from the Reverend Josiah Smith of Charleston which presented a very favorable impression of Whitefield: "He really appears to me, a Man of great Sincerity; to have a deep Sense of the Solemnities of our Religion, the highest Veneration for his Saviour, and the Zeal of a Seraph for the Honour of his great Master; and one that is no Stranger to the Worth of immortal Souls." Whitefield's commitment both to Calvinism and the doctrine of original sin also pleased Smith. The response in the *South-Carolina Gazette* to both Whitefield's preaching and Smith's letter was swift. "Laicus" appeared in the *Gazette* on January 19, 1740, expressing mock concern that a ball would be held in Charleston when "Mourning and Humiliation" were more appropriate. On January 26, the *Gazette* printed a response to Smith from "Arminius." Arminius was most likely South Carolina Commissary Alexander Garden, the highest-ranking Anglican in the colony and an opponent of Whitefield.[80] Arminius attacked Whitefield as a haughty zealot as well as Smith for his unquestioning support of Whitefield: "They extol his Person as some thing more than Human, and triumph in his Performances, which they praise, as inimitable." Arminius continued his argument in the next two issues of the *Gazette* (February 2 and 9), while

Smith answered back in eight nonconsecutive issues.[81] An anonymous contributor attacked Smith in the *Gazette* on October 23. In all, the argument ran one week short of a full year, ending on January 15, 1741, with Smith informing readers that his argument with Arminius would soon be available in pamphlet form. Sixteen separate items appeared in the *South-Carolina Gazette* on the controversy, contributed by four different writers.

On January 22, 1741, one week after the conclusion of Smith's battle with Arminius, Smith contributed to the *Gazette* excerpts of letters he had received from ministers in and around Boston which lauded Whitefield's preaching in New England. Two months later on March 19, 1741, the *Gazette* reprinted a positive report of Gilbert Tennent's New England preaching tour from the *New England Weekly Journal* for February 10. All this proved too much for one Anglican reader of the *Gazette*, who in a June 18 postscript offered his own extracts of four letters from New England which presented very different opinions of Whitefield and Tennent. Over the next four months, ten additional letters appeared as seven different contributors battled under pseudonyms such as Philalethes, Philanthropos, Philaretes, and Zealot the Second.[82] No other region of the colonies experienced such lengthy paper wars with so many different contributors.

In terms of tone, the primary local paper wars in the *South-Carolina Gazette* were similar to those found in the Boston papers in that the attacks were often personal, vituperative, and sarcastic. When one examines the issues discussed in these battles, however, differences emerge. While Bostonians argued over topics that dealt with religious tradition and church stability, the most lengthy local paper wars in the South dealt more with theological matters. For example, contributors to the paper war of 1740 between Smith and Arminius actually used very little newspaper space to discuss Whitefield and instead used significant space to debate the concept of original sin and Calvinist versus Arminian doctrine. For example, Arminius complained that Whitefield had come to South Carolina to expound on the "old and exploded Doctrines of Calvinism, to the no small Pleasure of the Party." Arminius also utilized two of his contributions to attempt

to refute the doctrine of original sin. Smith used five of his install-
ments to defend the doctrine of original sin, quoting such disparate
writers as the New Testament author James, Virgil, and John Milton
to prove his point.

Similarly, the paper war of 1741 is noteworthy mostly for the participants' divergence in their basic theological understanding of Christianity. On one side, contributors such as Philanthropos and Philaretes
argued for a reasonable Christianity, acceptable to the rational mind.
Their view is clear in Philanthropos' letter of October 3: "But, answer
me yee Zealots, can there be any such Thing as a Religion, truly and
properly so called, that is not rational? Is not Religion founded on the
Reason and Nature of Things, and must it not then be rational? What
is it that makes yee, if in Truth yee are, Christians, rather than Maho-
metans? And see, if Reason is not the principal Thing in the Case. If
it is not, yee may e'en as well be at once circumcis'd, and preach to
us next from the Alcoran." On September 19, Philaretes used his four-
page letter to denounce Whitefield as a "Brain-sick Prophet" and to
criticize contributors Josiah Smith and Zealot the Second for attacking
"Reason and a rational Religion."

On the other side, Smith and Zealot the Second defended a religion
of the heart and derided Philanthropos and those like him for being
"Gentlemen of Sense" who practice "Religion animated with the least
Degree of pious Fervency, with but a spark of sacred Passion" (July
23). In the same letter, Zealot the Second complained of Philanthropos'
inferior "rational Religion." Thus, the paper wars of the South applied
the passion of Boston contributors to theological issues related to understanding the very fundamentals of Christianity.

Historian Frank Lambert has noted that the newspaper debates over
the Awakening successfully moved religion from the private arena into
the public,[83] while journalism scholars Sloan and Williams identify colonial newspapers as giving "form to the scattered threads of emotional
religious outbursts in the colonies."[84] What is unique to each region of
the colonies, however, is how these debates were conducted as well as
the topics discussed, as newspaper readers brought their own opinions
and interpretations to the religious events of the 1740s.

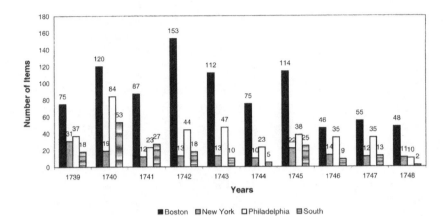

Figure 2.1. *Regional Comparison of All Newspapers*

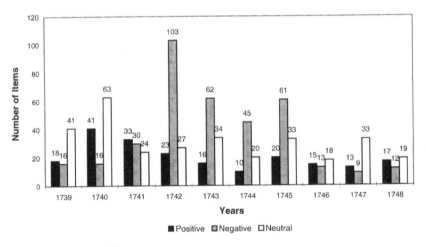

Figure 2.2. *Boston Newspapers*

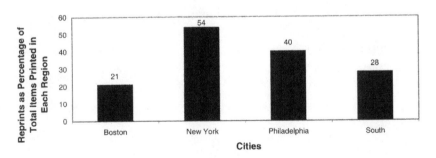

Figure 2.3. *Reprint Percentages by Region, Reprints Produced by Region*

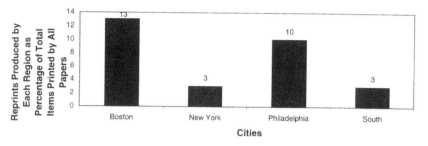

Figure 2.3. *(Continued)*

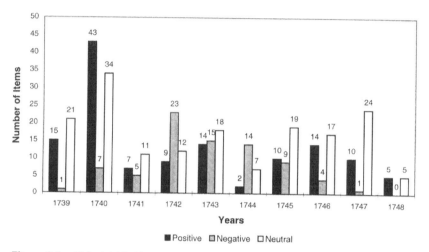

Figure 2.4. *Philadelphia Newspapers*

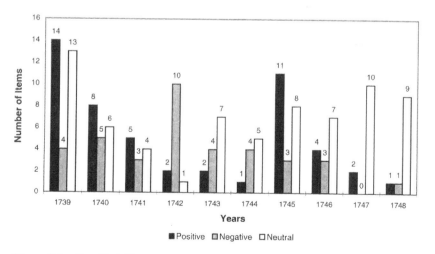

Figure 2.5. *New York Newspapers*

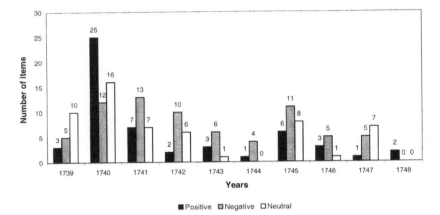

Figure 2.6. Southern Newspapers

NOTES

1. *Boston Gazette*, September 13, 1748.

2. Because of the lack of extant copies of the *Virginia Gazette*, it is unknown if the story was reprinted in Virginia.

3. Again, it is unknown if the story was reprinted in the *Virginia Gazette*.

4. Lambert, *Inventing*, 119. See this work for more on the idea of preparation for revival.

5. By 1741, all but one of the twelve colonial newspapers were under the ownership of their printers (Charles E. Clark, "Part I. Early American Journalism: News and Opinion in the Popular Press," in *The Colonial Book in the Atlantic World*, eds. Hugh Amory and David D. Hall, vol. 1, *A History of the Book in America*, 347-66 [Cambridge, MA: Cambridge University Press, 2000], 356).

6. Brown, *Knowledge*, 79.

7. Of these, a small percentage were poems or excerpts from published works.

8. As noted above, almost 50 percent, or 191, of the 387 negative letters appeared in Thomas Fleet's anti-revival *Boston Evening-Post*.

9. The public print debate over the revival was well-distributed and well-crafted. James N. Green has noted the effectiveness of the printed record of the movement: "The pamphlets generated by the political controversies of the 1720s were crude libels or pompous proclamations that even at the time must have been unintelligible to someone not part of the local gossip network. By

contrast, the books and pamphlets generated by the Great Awakening lucidly debated all the issues, so that the entire episode on some level was represented in print and could be apprehended at a distance." Green, "English Books and Printing," 261.

10. Almost 60 percent of all contributed letters were about or written by well-known revivalists Whitefield, Tennent, and Davenport and thus were transcolonial in their appeal. These controversies are discussed in depth in chapter 3.

11. See Lambert, *Inventing*, chapter 2, for a discussion of the Northampton revival and New England's expectation of periodic revivals.

12. Thomas, *History of Printing*, 8.

13. No other colonial city printed even half as many items on the revival during the ten-year period spanning Whitefield's two American preaching tours, 1739-1748. Most of the items were printed by five Boston papers—*Boston Evening-Post, Boston Gazette, Boston Weekly News-Letter, Boston Weekly Post-Boy*, and *New England Weekly Journal*. Gamaliel Rogers and Daniel Fowle began the *Independent Advertiser* in Boston in 1748; the paper printed nine items on the revival in 1748, all but one of which were positive or neutral, but missed the bulk of reporting on the revival.

14. The *Maryland Gazette*, the only newspaper in Maryland, had a reprint percentage of only 14 percent, but the *Gazette* printed a total of only seven items on the revival.

15. See Lambert, *Inventing*, 165-71, for a discussion of how the *Christian History* and other revival magazines helped create a sense of a "great" Awakening. See also Susan Durden, "A Study of the First Evangelical Magazines, 1740-1748," *Journal of Ecclesiastical History* 27 (1976): 255-75, for a discussion of the *Christian History* in an international context.

16. Michael J. Crawford, *Seasons of Grace: Colonial New England's Revival Tradition in Its British Context* (Oxford, England: Oxford University Press, 1991), 184. Crawford provides a complete list of revival narratives written and printed between 1741 and 1745 in Appendix 2. The narratives by William Shurtleff, Henry Messinger and Elias Haven, Jonathan Edwards, Joseph Park, William Tennent, Jr., and Thomas Prince were also published in *The Christian Monthly History* (Edinburgh). Samuel Blair's narrative was also published as *A Short and Faithful Narrative of the Late Remarkable Revival of Religion in the Congregation of New-Londonderry, and Other Parts of Pennsylvania* (Philadelphia, 1744). John Rowland's account "A Narrative of the Revival and Progress of Religion, in the Towns of Hopewell, Amwell and Maiden-Head, in New-Jersey, and New-Providence in Pennsylvania," the only narrative not published in *The Christian History*, is the second title in Gilbert

Tennent's *A Funeral Sermon Occasion'd by the Death of . . . John Rowland* (Philadelphia, 1745), 49-72.

17. The *Christian History* appeared in the *Boston Evening-Post* on March 7, March 14, April 4, April 30, July 4, October 10, October 24, and December 12, 1743; January 16, February 13, February 27, March 26, August 27, and October 15, 1744; and March 25, 1745. Other appearances of the *History* were in the *Boston Weekly News-Letter* on March 17, 1743, and the *Boston Gazette* on June 28, 1743.

18. *Boston Evening-Post*, March 26, 1744.

19. Clifford K. Shipton, *Sibley's Harvard Graduates*, 14 vols. (Boston, MA: Harvard University Press, 1933-1975), 10:534.

20. In 1741, both Benjamin Franklin and Andrew Bradford attempted to begin magazines in Philadelphia, but failed, with Bradford's *American Magazine, or a Monthly View* lasting only three issues and Franklin's *General Magazine, and Historical Chronicle, For all the British Plantations in America* only six. Gamaliel Rogers' and Daniel Fowle's *Boston Weekly Magazine* mentioned above began in March 1743 as did the *Christian History*, but it lasted only four weeks.

21. Frank Luther Mott, *A History of American Magazines, 1741-1850*, vol. 1 (New York: D. Appleton and Company, 1930), 25, 71-82, and Lyon N. Richardson, *A History of Early American Magazines, 1741-1789* (New York: Thomas Nelson and Sons, 1931), 58-73.

22. Draper printed seventy-five news reports and sixty-one letters during 1739-1748. Two-thirds of Draper's news reports were neutral, with the positive and negative reports split almost equally. Of the letters he printed, twenty were positive, twenty-eight were negative, and thirteen were neutral. Draper doubled his coverage of the movement from 1739 to 1740, jumping from sixteen notices to thirty. Although printing only thirteen items in 1741, he printed twenty-nine items in 1742.

23. For most years, the coverage in Huske's paper was predominantly neutral. Exceptions were the years 1741 and 1742, when controversy regarding the Awakening was at its height, and the *Post-Boy*'s negative coverage exceeded positive. The *Post-Boy* printed almost equal numbers of news reports and letters, although no letters regarding the revival appeared after 1743.

24. Kneeland and Green also worked with Thomas Prince, Jr., to print the revivalist magazine *The Christian History*. As historian Isaiah Thomas writes of the *Boston Gazette*, "The printers of this paper were great advocates of the reverend George Whitefield, the reverend Mr. Edwards, &c. The reverend Thomas Prince was supposed to have taken an active part in the publication

of this paper, and for a time to have assisted in correcting the press." Thomas, *History of Printing*, 245.

25. The *Boston Gazette* printed the next highest number of items on the revival with 203, and, when combined with the 104 items printed in the *New England Weekly Journal*, the total becomes 307 items for printers Kneeland and Green, still slightly less than the number published by Fleet in the *Post*. However, many issues of the *Boston Gazette* are not extant for the years 1741 and 1742, so the actual number of items printed by the *Gazette* is probably higher.

26. Letters constituted approximately 53 percent of coverage by the *American Weekly Mercury* and *Boston Weekly Post-Boy*, and almost 66 percent of reporting by the *South-Carolina Gazette*.

27. The other newspaper publishing in Boston at the end of Whitefield's second preaching tour, noted above, was the *Independent Advertiser*. Nine news items on the revival appeared in the *Advertiser* in 1748—six were positive, one was negative, and two were neutral.

28. The Rev. John Brown served the First Congregational Church in Haverhill, Massachusetts, less than twenty miles from Newbury, and may have been the author of this letter.

29. The letters can be found in the *Boston Evening-Post* for June 10 (a response to an earlier call for a doctrinal statement of the revival); August 12, 19 (2), 26 (2); and September 2, 16 (2), 23, 1745.

30. See Schmidt, *Hearing Things*, 41, for a short discussion of the basis of opposition to itinerant preaching.

31. For letters in the *Boston Evening-Post,* see May 3, May 24, and July 5, 1742; for letters in the *Boston Gazette*, see May 18 and June 29, 1742.

32. Letters appeared in the *Boston Gazette* (November 30, 1742), *Boston Evening-Post* (December 20 and December 27, 1742; January 31, 1743), and *Boston Weekly News-Letter* (December 30, 1742; January 6, January 20, and January 27, 1743).

33. According to Frank Lambert, forty-two Separate congregations arose in New England between the years 1741 and 1745 (*Inventing*, 245).

34. The February 26, 1745, issue of the *Boston Gazette* is not extant.

35. *Boston Gazette*, April 7.

36. Rogers, November 22, 1742; Buell, November 29, 1742; Adams, April 6, 1747; Conant, April 15, 1745; Leavitt, October 28, 1745.

37. Croswell's role in the revival was significant; as Leigh Eric Schmidt has noted, "Croswell was more persistent and visible, provoked more controversies, itinerated longer, and published more tracts than any other incendiary

New Light, including James Davenport" (Schmidt, "'A Second and Glorious Reformation': The New Light Extremism of Andrew Croswell," *The William and Mary Quarterly*, 3rd ser., 43 [1986]: 214-44.) Biographical information on Croswell is from Jacob C. Meyer, *Church and State in Massachusetts from 1740 to 1833: A Chapter in the History of the Development of Individual Freedom* (Cleveland, OH: Case Western Reserve University Press, 1930), 26; Shipton, *Sibley's Harvard Graduates*, 8:387, 390, 396-97; and Heimert and Miller, *Crisis and Consequences*, 505-6.

38. Sixteenth-century theologian Jacobus Arminius opposed the Calvinist teaching of predestination and emphasized the role of human free will in salvation. Those who espouse this doctrine are called Arminians.

39. When Davenport entered Boston for a preaching tour in June 1742, he met with the associated ministers and they concluded from Davenport's answers to their questions that he was a "truly pious" man, but that they could not condone his propensity to act upon "sudden Impulses," his singing in the public streets, and his encouragement of lay preaching. The ministers therefore refused Davenport access to their pulpits, yet affirmed "the great and glorious Work of God, which of his free Grace he has begun and is carrying on in many Parts of this and the neighboring Provinces." Davenport's preaching tour of Boston is discussed in detail in chapter 3.

40. Edwin Scott Gaustad, *The Great Awakening in New England* (New York: Harper & Brothers, 1957), 149n; William Buell Sprague, *Annals of the American Pulpit*, 9 vols. (New York: R. Carter and Brothers, 1857-1869), 3:44.

41. Moorhead made other unspecified charges against Caldwell and declared he could prove his claim in court. When Caldwell brought a suit against Moorhead in the Inferiour Court of Common Pleas on July 6, 1742, the jury awarded Caldwell 250 £. Moorhead appealed the judgment to the Superiour Court of Judicature. According to Barney L. Jones, Moorhead's appeal came before the Superiour Court one year later on August 16, 1743, but because Caldwell failed to appear in court, the Chief Justice reversed the decision (179). Barney L. Jones, "John Caldwell, Critic of the Great Awakening in New England," in *A Miscellany of American Christianity: Essays in Honor of H. Shelton Smith*, ed. Stuart C. Henry, 168-82 (Durham, NC: Duke University Press, 1963), 177.

42. Moorhead's questionable writing style is apparent from the first sentences of his December 27, 1742, letter to the *Boston Evening-Post*: "Having lately seen a late News-Paper I read therein a long Letter of some Synonimous Author, for all his fictious Letters. Soon after I had read it I presently foresaw

it was designed against me and my Advertisement, and therefore thought it my Duty to write an Answer to it."

43. Foxcroft's pamphlet was published during Whitefield's second colonial preaching tour and was in response to *A Letter to the Reverend Mr. George Whitefield, publickly calling upon him to vindicate his conduct, or confess his faults* (Boston, 1744), authored by L. K. (possibly Charles Chauncy). The letters against Foxcroft appeared in the *Boston Evening-Post* on February 4, February 11, February 25, March 25, April 1, and June 3, 1745.

44. For more detail on the Scottish revival style, see Lambert, *Inventing*, 61ff., and Westerkamp, "Enthusiastic Piety."

45. Lambert, *Inventing*, 55-57, 61. See Archibald Alexander, *Biographical Sketches of the Founder, and Principal Alumni of the Log College* (Princeton, 1845) for more on the Log College, and Coalter, *Gilbert Tennent*, for more on Gilbert Tennent and his family.

46. Charles Hartshorn Maxson, *The Great Awakening in the Middle Colonies* (Chicago, IL: University of Chicago Press, 1920), 33.

47. See Stout, *Divine Dramatist*, 89, for a short discussion of Philadelphia at the time of Whitefield's arrival.

48. Frank Lambert, "Subscribing for Profits and Piety: The Friendship of Benjamin Franklin and George Whitefield," *The William and Mary Quarterly*, 3rd ser., 50 (1993): 529, 544, 538. See J. A. Leo Lemay, *The Life of Benjamin Franklin, Volume 2* (Philadelphia: University of Pennsylvania Press, 2006), 424ff., for a discussion of Franklin's role as Whitefield's primary colonial printer.

49. J. A. Leo Lemay, *The Life of Benjamin Franklin, Volume 1* (Philadelphia: University of Pennsylvania Press, 2006), 209-10.

50. See Lemay, *Life*, 2: 23-25, for a discussion of Franklin's religious views.

51. Lemay and Zall, *Autobiography of Benjamin Franklin*, 105-6.

52. For more on the personal and professional aspects of Franklin and Whitefield's relationship, see Lambert, "Profits and Piety," 529-54, and Kerry S. Walters, *Benjamin Franklin and His Gods* (Urbana, IL: University of Illinois Press, 1999), 142-45.

53. The *Mercury* was discontinued after 1746, although Thomas notes that some proof exists that the paper continued in 1749 (890). Like the *Mercury*, the *Boston Weekly News-Letter* also printed 136 items on the revival during the years 1739-1748.

54. A full discussion of the controversy over Whitefield's use of funds for his orphanage appears in chapter 3.

55. Lemay and Zall, *Autobiography of Benjamin Franklin*, 107.

56. For example, see J. M. Bumsted, *The Great Awakening: The Beginnings of Evangelical Pietism in America*, Primary Sources in American History (Waltham, MA: Blaisdell Publishing Company, 1970), 171-78, for an argument over whether or not Moravians could preach in the New Building erected for Whitefield in Philadelphia.

57. *Pennsylvania Gazette*, Postscript, July 24, 1740.

58. Lemay suggests that Kinnersley's breach with the Baptist church was probably healed by the fall, and Kinnersley remained an important member of the church, although it appears he was never offered a church of his own. J. A. Leo Lemay, *Ebenezer Kinnersley, Franklin's Friend* (Philadelphia: University of Pennsylvania Press, 1964), 36. For a detailed discussion of Kinnersley's sermon against Rowland and its repercussions, see 19-35.

59. Lambert, *Inventing*, 118.

60. Thomas, *History of Printing*, 487-90, mentions the trial; see also Stanley Nider Katz, ed. *A Brief Narrative of the Case and Trial of John Peter Zenger, Printer of* The New-York Weekly Journal, John Harvard Library (Cambridge, MA: Harvard University Press, Belknap Press, 1972), and Alison Olson, "The Zenger Case Revisited: Satire, Sedition and Political Debate in Eighteenth Century America," *Early American Literature* 35 (2000): 223-45.

61. *American National Biography*, 24 vols. (New York: Oxford University Press, 1999), 17:27-28; see also Alan Dyer, *A Biography of James Parker, Colonial Printer* (New York: Whitson Publishing Co., 1982).

62. In my calculations, I have treated Parker's *New-York Weekly Post-Boy* and *New-York Gazette* as one paper.

63. Figure 2.6 reveals the number and tone of revival-related newspaper items in the southern colonies of Maryland, Virginia, and South Carolina.

64. J. A. Leo Lemay, *Men of Letters in Colonial Maryland* (Knoxville: University of Tennessee Press, 1982), 321.

65. William Parks of Maryland had begun the *Maryland Gazette* in 1727, but ceased printing it in 1734 as Parks was then residing in Virginia.

66. *American National Biography*, 9:498-99. See Lemay, *Men of Letters*, 193-212, for more on Green as a printer and man of letters.

67. Alexander Hamilton, *The History of the Ancient and Honorable Tuesday Club*, ed. Robert Micklus, 3 vols. (Chapel Hill: University of North Carolina Press, 1990), 118.

68. Hamilton, *Tuesday Club*, 202.

69. Wesley M. Gewehr, *The Great Awakening in Virginia, 1740-1790* (Durham, NC: Duke University Press, 1930), 26-27; Lambert, *Inventing*, 140ff. See John K. Nelson, *A Blessed Company: Parishes, Parsons, and Pa-*

rishioners in Anglican Virginia, 1690-1776 (Chapel Hill: The University of North Carolina Press, 2001) for an extended discussion of the everyday world of Virginian Anglicanism.

70. In 1729, Parks printed the "Plain-Dealer" essay series in his *Maryland Gazette*, a combination of original and borrowed essays with a deistic slant (Lemay, *Men of Letters*, 115-18). For more on Parks, see *American National Biography*, 17:56-58; Lawrence C. Wroth, *William Parks: Printer and Journalist of England and Colonial America* (Richmond, VA: Appeals Press, 1926); and Lemay, *Men of Letters*, 111-25.

71. William Howland Kenney, III, "Alexander Garden and George Whitefield: The Significance of Revivalism in South Carolina, 1738-1741," *South Carolina Historical Magazine* 71 (1970): 7.

72. Franklin writes, "She not only present[ed] me as clear an Account as she could find of the Transactions past, but continu'd to account with the greatest Regularity and Exactitude every Quarter afterwards; and manag'd the Business with such Success that she not only brought up reputably a Family of Children, but at the Expiration of the Term was able to purchase of me the Printing-House and establish her Son in it." Lemay and Zall, *Autobiography of Benjamin Franklin*, 95-96.

73. *American National Biography*, 21:689-91; Thomas, *History of Printing*, 567-69. For Elizabeth Timothy, see also Madelon Golden Schilpp and Sharon M. Murphy, *Great Women of the Press*, New Horizons in Journalism (Carbondale, IL: Southern Illinois University Press, 1983), and Ira L. Baker, "Elizabeth Timothy: America's First Woman Editor," *Journalism Quarterly* 54 (1977): 280-85. Also helpful is Hennig Cohen, *The South-Carolina Gazette, 1732-1775* (Columbia: University of South Carolina Press, 1953), 238-41. For editorial policies of the *Gazette*, see Jeffery A. Smith, "Impartiality and Revolutionary Ideology: Editorial Policies of the *South-Carolina Gazette, 1732-1775*," *Journal of Southern History* 49 (1983): 511-26.

74. The reprint rate of the *Maryland Gazette* was actually the second lowest in the colonies at 14 percent, but a total of only seven items on the revival were printed by that paper.

75. Items from the *Pennsylvania Gazette* were reprinted the most times (88), followed by the *Boston Evening-Post* (76) and the *Boston Gazette* (57).

76. In reality, the suspension had little effect on Whitefield. See Edward McCrady, *The History of South Carolina Under the Royal Government, 1719-1776* (1899; repr., New York: Russell & Russell-Atheneum, 1969), 234-38; Luke Tyerman, *The Life of the Rev. George Whitefield*, 2 vols. (London: Hodder and Stoughton, 1876), 1:395-402; and Kenney, III, "Alexander Garden,"

1-16. See Whitefield's journal for March 14, July 13, July 19, and July 20, 1740, for his version of the events in Charleston.

77. On May 5, 1746, the *South-Carolina Gazette* published affidavits concerning the affair, and on November 16, 1747, *Gazette* contributor W. R. asked Whitefield to respond to the affidavits. Nothing else regarding the case appeared in the *Gazette*, although the *Gazette* was not exhaustively examined after 1748.

78. Benjamin Franklin reprinted Bryan's letter from the *South-Carolina Gazette* in his *General Magazine and Historical Chronicle* for March 1741 (Benjamin Franklin, *The General Magazine and Historical Chronicle*, vol. 1, no. 3 [New York: Columbia University Press, 1938], 202-5).

79. McCrady, *History of South Carolina*, 241.

80. For a discussion of the controversy between Josiah Smith and Arminius, see Cohen, *South-Carolina Gazette*, 222. For more on Smith's involvement with the revival, see Shipton, *Sibley's Harvard Graduates*, 7:577.

81. On February 2, Smith promised a response in the *Gazette* to Arminius' comments. Smith's lengthy answer appeared in the following issues of the *South-Carolina Gazette*: February 9 and 16; March 1, 15, and 22; July 1; August 30; and October 2, 1740.

82. The additional letters appeared in the following issues of the *South-Carolina Gazette*: June 25 (2); July 23; September 19 and 26; October 3 (2), 10, and 17, 1741 (2). Many letters on further controversies appeared in the *South-Carolina Gazette* during Whitefield's second preaching tour of the colonies, but they tended to have intercolonial significance and will be discussed in chapter 3.

83. Frank Lambert, *Pedlar in Divinity: George Whitefield and the Transatlantic Revivals, 1737-1770* (Princeton: Princeton UP, 1994), 170.

84. Wm. David Sloan and Julie Hedgepeth Williams, *The Early American Press, 1690-1783*, The History of American Journalism 1 (Westport, CT: Greenwood Press, 1994), 108.

Whitefield, Tennent, and Davenport: Newsmakers of the Awakening

Blame us not if we still continue to esteem you a mercenary self-seeking Man, all whose Pretence to Godliness, when discovered and laid open to the Bottom, is mere Hypocrisy, in order to get Money and popular Applause. Another hot-headed, ambitious Phantom, who under Pretence of bringing New Light into the Firmament of the Church, hath set her in a Flame wherever you come, or at least have endeavored to do so, and by so doing have exposed yourself to the Danger of being Thunder-struck with divine Vengeance.

Letter from "Plain-Dealing" to George Whitefield, October 1745[1]

I have found the advantage of the things my adversaries have inserted in the public papers: they do but excite people's curiosity, and serve to raise their attention.

George Whitefield, 1739 (*George Whitefield's Journals*, 373)

On board the *Elizabeth* in August 1739, traveling to the American colonies for his first preaching tour, George Whitefield wrote *A Short Account of God's Dealings with the Reverend Mr. George Whitefield*. Emotional, personal, and often dramatic, Whitefield's *Short Account* describes the events of the evangelist's life from his birth until his ordination in the Church of England and offers detailed descriptions of seminal moments in his spiritual life. Although just twenty-five years old, Whitefield knew how to write a fetching tale; here, he describes his conversion while at Pembroke College after suffering under much "soul-distress" for many months:

> After I had been groaning under an unspeakable pressure both of body and mind for above a twelve-month, God was pleased to set me free in the following manner. One day, perceiving an uncommon drought and a disagreeable clamminess in my mouth and using things to allay my thirst, but in vain, it was suggested to me, that when Jesus Christ cried out, "I thirst," His sufferings were near at an end. Upon which I cast myself down on the bed, crying out, "I thirst! I thirst!" Soon after this, I found and felt in myself that I was delivered from the burden that had so heavily oppressed me. The spirit of mourning was taken from me, and I knew what it was truly to rejoice in God my Saviour; and, for some time, could not avoid singing psalms wherever I was. (58)

Whitefield published his *Short Account* in both England and America in 1740, authorizing five editions in Great Britain and five in the colonies.[2] Colonial readers were so taken with the work that it has been estimated that ten times as many copies, under the new title *A Brief and General Account of the Life of the Rev. George Whitefield*, were printed in the colonies as were in England.[3] In fact, Whitefield authored more printed works than anyone else in the colonies from 1731 through 1750.[4] Frank Lambert estimates that between 1737 and 1745, one copy of a Whitefield publication was available for every eleven colonists.[5]

The popularity of Whitefield's *Short Account* as well as writings by other revivalists reveals the recognition many clergymen achieved during the revival years. Some ministers such as New England clergymen Jonathan Edwards and Charles Chauncy became known for their polemical works which attempted to define, defend, or critique the religious events of the time. Other clergymen received local attention for their preaching, particularly if it was itinerant. Even the occasional layman received notoriety as did planter Hugh Bryan in South Carolina for his dire predictions of Charleston's destruction.

Whitefield's deliberate efforts to create a popular image in the colonies have been well-documented by scholars such as Harry S. Stout, who identifies Whitefield as "Anglo-America's first modern celebrity."[6] Whitefield's judicious use of the press and his own strength of personality gained him national attention in both the colonies and the

British Isles.[7] Whitefield printed his more popular sermons, chronicled his religious experiences in published journals, and even employed follower William Seward as a press agent of sorts. Seward fed news items to the local newspapers which reported on Whitefield's preaching successes and alerted readers to the evangelist's upcoming meetings.

The weekly colonial newspapers played their part in making household names of various revivalists. Newspapers were uniquely positioned to function as celebrity-making machines. The fact that the papers appeared throughout the colonies weekly, had a broad readership, and included reprints from other papers as a matter of course ensured that those whose names appeared often would receive some measure of intercolonial fame. As noted above, Whitefield realized early in his ministry the advantages of appearing in the newspapers and worked intentionally to make that happen.

While coverage of no other single revivalist compares with the print attention afforded Whitefield, two American revivalists did gain some measure of intercolonial fame—Presbyterian Gilbert Tennent and Congregationalist James Davenport. Figure 3.1 reveals that while Whitefield was clearly the most popular revivalist according to the papers, Tennent and Davenport did appear frequently during key years of the movement (see figures at the end of this chapter). Tennent's hellfire-and-brimstone preaching and Davenport's unusual public antics ensured that each man's itinerant preaching tours throughout New England and the Middle Colonies received sufficient newspaper coverage to grant him "celebrity" status. Interestingly, individuals often associated in modern minds with the revival, such as New England proponent Jonathan Edwards and Boston revival critic Charles Chauncy, do not appear in the newspapers, except for advertisements for works they authored. The probable reason for this omission is that while both Edwards and Chauncy authored popular writings on the revival, neither man traveled throughout the colonies preaching. The physical presence of men such as Whitefield and Tennent outside of their home churches obviously gave them greater visibility and thus increased popularity.

The newspapers made Whitefield, Tennent, and Davenport household names in several ways. First, the preaching tours of each were covered by the papers in close detail. Whitefield's tours of 1739-1741 and 1744-1748 were of course reported on very heavily, but news reports were also consistent for the tours of Tennent (New England, 1740-1741) and Davenport (Connecticut, 1741 and 1742; Massachusetts, 1742). Also reported by the papers were significant events in each man's ministry, such as Tennent's doubts regarding the direction of the revival and Davenport's fanatical book-burning incident in New London, Connecticut. Even Tennent's second marriage was noted by the papers. Of the 837 news reports on the revival in the papers during the years 1739-1748, almost 80 percent were about Whitefield (73 percent), Tennent (3 percent), and Davenport (3 percent).

The papers also printed numerous contributed letters concerning the clergymen. While Whitefield received by far the most reader commentary, Tennent and Davenport appeared often as the subjects of accusatory or appreciative letters during their itinerant travels. In addition, letters by the men, though not many in number, were among the few letters from prominent revivalists to appear consistently in the papers. Fifty-nine percent of the 761 letters contributed to the newspapers during those years were about or by Whitefield (46 percent), Tennent (7 percent), and Davenport (6 percent). A poet in the *New-York Weekly Journal* for July 12, 1742, revealed the notoriety of the three clergymen when he quipped:

> Three Preachers in three different Places born,
> Georgia, New-Brunswick, Southold did adorn,
> The first to strike the Passions did excell [Whitefield],
> The next was fam'd for sending Souls to Hell [Tennent],
> The last had nothing of his own to show [Davenport],
> And therefore wisely join'd the former two.[8]

Unlike Whitefield, Tennent and Davenport did not appear to have a planned strategy for using the colonial newspapers to develop their public images. Yet, as reports and letters concerning their itinerant tours were printed, a public persona for each revivalist did emerge in the papers. While intentional efforts such as Whitefield's could influence how a revivalist appeared in the papers, since the newspapers were ostensibly open to all who wished to contribute, the revivalists had much less control over how they were presented and perceived in the papers than they did in other forms of print. Printers chose which news reports and letters to include in the papers, and contributors gave their own opinions and eye-witness accounts of each revivalist.

When one examines the presentation of these three revivalists in the newspapers, one shared characteristic that emerges is the variable nature of their public personas. Each revivalist experienced dramatic shifts in how he was presented by the papers during the most contentious years of the Awakening. Each revivalist handled these shifts differently, and each had a varying degree of success in molding his public image into what he desired it to be.

GEORGE WHITEFIELD

Born in the inn owned by his parents in Gloucester, England, Whitefield later called himself a perpetrator of "endless . . . sins and offences" as an adolescent.[9] Fond of playreading and acting, Whitefield's oratorical skills were recognized by his schoolteachers. His family's decreasing fortunes made a university education unattainable, so Whitefield quit his studies early in his teens and worked in his parents' inn for more than a year. During this time, Whitefield began to read the Bible frequently and composed several sermons. At eighteen, Whitefield entered Pembroke College, Oxford, paying his expenses by working as a college servitor. After a year of diligent study and strenuous religious exercises, Whitefield made the acquaintance of Charles Wesley. Following Wesley's advice, Whitefield read Henry Scougal's *The Life of God in the Soul of Man* and was shocked to read Scougal's assertion that religious works such as fasting and giving to the poor did not constitute "true religion"; on the contrary, Whitefield noted in his journal that "true religion was union of the soul with God, and Christ formed within us" (47). Upon reading Scougal's words, Whitefield experienced what he would call the "New Birth": "a ray of Divine light was instantaneously darted in upon my soul, and from that moment, but not till then, did I know that I must be a new creature" (47). Whitefield would later be known for his preaching on the New Birth.[10] From this time, Whitefield aligned himself with the followers of Anglican clergymen Charles and John Wesley, called Methodists because of the rigor with which they regulated their time and affairs.

In the spring of 1736, Whitefield received his bachelor's degree from Oxford and was ordained in June by Martin Benson, the Bishop of Gloucester. He began to minister at Oxford in place of Charles and John Wesley, who had traveled to the colony of Georgia as missionaries. Whitefield preached in Gloucester, Bristol, and London as well, speaking extemporaneously, passionately and dramatically emphasizing the New Birth, and using his body and voice to engage his listeners.[11] His unrivaled preaching, combining entertainment and theology, drew thousands. Sometimes, he preached nine times in a week. Whitefield quickly became a popular and influential leader in the religious movement begun by John and Charles Wesley in England and Howell Harris in Wales, which emphasized evangelical doctrine and experiential piety and which many contemporaries viewed as a genuine religious revival.

On December 28, 1737, Whitefield embarked aboard the *Whitaker* for Georgia, where he preached and visited the sick for four months. While there, Whitefield founded an orphanage in Savannah named Bethesda, or House of Mercy, for which he would preach and raise money throughout his life. When he returned to England, he became a fully licensed minister of the Church of England and received the Savannah orphanage and its surrounding areas as his parish. He immediately began preaching throughout England, raising money for the orphan house and attracting crowds that ranged from several hundred listeners to twenty thousand. Confronted with the thousands who gathered to hear him and without a church building of his own, Whitefield began preaching in the fields. Not surprisingly, Whitefield also experienced opposition, as many clergymen were uncomfortable with his extemporaneous praying, passionate preaching, and experiential approach to religion.[12]

In the midst of his success in England, Whitefield decided to visit America again, this time to raise money for his orphanage among the wealthy colonists and to help spread the message of the English revival. He departed for America on August 14, 1739, on board the *Elizabeth* for his first preaching tour of the colonies. At the age of twenty-four, Whitefield had established himself as a religious sensation in England and as a leader of the revival there. The young evangelist would use many of the same publicity techniques he had perfected in England in the colonies, ensuring the spread of both his fame and the movement.

Of the 1598 newspapers items printed on the Awakening between 1739 and 1748, inclusive, fully 60 percent related to Whitefield. One cannot overstate the influence of the evangelist on newspaper reporting on the revival in the colonies. Whitefield's name appeared consistently in every single colonial newspaper during the 1740s. Figure 3.2 reveals the extensive coverage Whitefield received in the papers. Not surprisingly, he was the most popular in colonial newspapers when he was in the colonies on preaching tours. Forty percent of the total number of newspaper items on Whitefield appeared during his 1739-1741 preaching tour, while his 1744-1748 visit produced almost 40 percent as well.[13] He appeared in the Boston newspapers 445 times, accounting for approximately 46 percent of his total newspaper appearances. Three hundred fifty-four, or almost 80 percent, of the Boston appearances were in the *Boston Gazette* and *Boston Evening-Post*.[14] In the Philadelphia papers, Whitefield appeared 275 times, accounting for almost 30 percent of his total appearances. Whitefield's friend Benjamin Franklin printed 119 items on the evangelist in his *Pennsylvania Gazette*, while Franklin's long-distance partners Elizabeth and Peter Timothy printed 114 items in their *South-Carolina Gazette*.

Although Whitefield was a consistent feature in colonial newspapers during the 1740s, the way he was presented in the news was anything but static. His public image in the papers underwent significant changes during his first two preaching tours of the colonies. Initially, Whitefield appeared in the papers as an icon, a larger-than-life representation of the power and experience of the revival. In the three and one-half years between his colonial tours, Whitefield's image changed as detractors began to question his methods and motives. By his second colonial preaching tour, Whitefield's image in the papers was more nuanced, varied, and vulnerable than ever before.

Before Whitefield arrived in the colonies to preach and travel in October 1739, colonial papers reprinted items from English papers that presented the evangelist as exciting, popular, and charismatic. Specifically, these reprints tended to emphasize Whitefield's popularity most often, as well as his effects on listeners. For example, on

December 16, 1737, the *Virginia Gazette* reported on Whitefield's preaching in England: "On Sunday the Rev. Mr. Whitefield, who is much followed, and whose Preaching is so deservedly approved of, preached at Six in the Morning at Cornhill, at Eleven in the Tower, at Three in the Afternoon in Old Fifth-street, and at Five in the Evening at St. Clemente's-Danes, when every Church was so crowded, that Numbers were obliged to withdraw from want of Room." The report was reprinted by the *Boston Evening-Post* on January 2, 1738. The *New England Weekly Journal* for June 19, 1739, reprinted a notice that estimated the "innumerable multitude" at Whitefield's recent sermon in Moorfield at 20,000, with 30,000 listeners estimated later that day at Kennington Common. On July 12, 1739, the *Pennsylvania Gazette* noted that Whitefield had preached again at Kennington Common "to about 20,000 People, among whom were near forty Coaches, besides Chaises, and about one hundred on Horseback." The *American Weekly Mercury* informed Philadelphia readers on July 19, 1739, that Whitefield could draw crowds without even trying: "On Tuesday Night the Rev. Mr. Whitefield went to expound at a Society on Dowgate Hill, but finding two or three thousand People in the Street, he preach'd to them from the Shop-Window." In the South, the *South-Carolina Gazette* reprinted reports such as the one on July 14, 1739, that Whitefield was "preaching every Day to large Audiences, visiting, and expounding to religious Societies."

According to the reprints in the colonial papers, Whitefield's listeners were impressed and attentive. The *Boston Weekly News-Letter* for April 19 noted that in Kingswood, "tho' there was such a great Number of People, all was very quiet." Similarly, the *Pennsylvania Gazette* reprinted that while Whitefield preached to 20,000 people at Kennington Common, "an awful Silence was kept during the whole time of Singing, Prayers and Sermon." According to the *American Weekly Mercury* for July 12, 1739, even "Gentlemen and Persons of Distinction" flocked to hear the young evangelist. On April 19, 1739, the *Boston Weekly News-Letter* reprinted a London report that Whitefield was "very much esteemed by many in this City."

The opposition that Whitefield was already experiencing from the established church in England was noted by colonial papers before the evangelist arrived in the colonies, but was not emphasized. On June 25,

1739, the *Boston Gazette* reported that at one church, Whitefield had been "denied the Pulpit" by church officials and so had preached in the church graveyard. Both the *Pennsylvania Gazette* (July 5) and the *New-York Gazette* (July 9) reprinted the story. Colonial papers identified some who opposed the young preacher—Joseph Trapp, Henry Stebbing, the Bishop of Gloucester, and other ecclesiastical and governmental officials.[15] The *New England Weekly Journal* for July 24, 1739, noted the "Disgust" the civil authorities felt toward Whitefield, while the July 17, 1739, *Virginia Gazette* reported a rebuff Whitefield had received when attempting to preach in Oxford. However, before his arrival in the colonies, Whitefield's popularity among the masses certainly appeared more often in colonial papers than did his struggles. The *Boston Weekly News-Letter* reprinted a report that a "hot-headed Spark" risked his life when he dared to criticize Whitefield "among the Mob" (July 19, 1739).

Whitefield's positive image in the papers even before his first colonial preaching tour is not surprising when one considers how prepared colonial readers were to receive Whitefield. As in England, increased religious activity in the colonies had been occurring for some years. Congregational minister Jonathan Edwards had declared that revival had come to his Northampton, Massachusetts, church in the mid-1730s as he preached the doctrines of justification by faith. In the Middle Colonies, the Rev. William Tennent's Log College was training Presbyterian revivalist preachers, while Dutch Reformed clergyman Theodore Frelinghuysen had been successfully preaching the New Birth and experiential piety for twenty years in New Jersey.[16] Gerald Moran asserts that church participation in Connecticut had been growing consistently since the early 1680s.[17]

This interest in the evangelical brand of Christianity that Whitefield represented certainly paved the way for the young preacher as he came to the colonies for his first preaching tour. On July 17, 1739, the *New England Weekly Journal* noted Whitefield's planned voyage to America: "On Saturday Afternoon the Rev. Mr. Whitefield went on board the Elizabeth, Capt. Allen, bound for Philadelphia, (he designing to call there in his Way to Georgia) and agreed for the Passage of himself and Friends, and to leave London this Day three Weeks." Thus, when Whitefield arrived in Philadelphia in November 1739, colonial newspaper readers expected a powerful and exciting orator.

Whitefield as Icon: First Preaching Tour, October 1739-January 1741

On October 30, 1739, at the age of twenty-four, Whitefield arrived at Lewes, now in Delaware, for his first preaching tour of the American colonies. His first tour would last until January 1741, during which time he would preach in every colony during his stay and would unite colonial revivalists in their pursuit of a general revival of religion. He would command widespread coverage in colonial newspapers, appearing 390 times during his tour. His name would become a household word in the colonies.

Whitefield's image in the colonial papers during his first preaching tour can be summed up as iconic. He appeared more as a symbol of the religious events of the time and less as a man. While his published journals revealed much of his personal thoughts and spirituality, his coverage in the newspapers was more two-dimensional, focusing instead on his preaching travels and accomplishments. He functioned in the papers as a representative of the revival, providing for both supporters and detractors an individual onto whom they could project their hopes and fears for colonial Christianity.

One aspect of Whitefield's iconic image in the papers was the remarkably widespread and frequent coverage he received. Reporting was consistent and extensive, with every paper in the cities he visited reporting on the evangelist. As noted above, 390 reports appeared on Whitefield in the papers during his first preaching tour, significantly more than any other person or event in those years. Papers from other colonies also consistently reprinted reports from the host cities throughout Whitefield's first tour. In fact, more than 40 percent of all items printed on Whitefield and the revival during Whitefield's first tour were reprints. In this way, readers throughout the colonies followed Whitefield's progress.

Sixty-four percent, or 248, of these newspaper items were "news" reports which offered readers factual information on the evangelist. These reports had little or no explicit opinion attached, although in terms of tone, most of these items were implicitly positive or neutral. In terms of content, the news reports presented logistical information such as number of listeners, amount of money Whitefield collected, and planned itinerary. Whitefield's reception by his listeners was also noted, with emphasis on audience reaction and, often, the social class of those who attended his preaching.

The coverage of Whitefield's first preaching stop by the Philadelphia newspapers is representative of news reports throughout the colonies during Whitefield's first tour. Whitefield's began his first colonial preaching tour in Philadelphia, where he met briefly with clergymen to explain his ministry and mission, then read prayers and preached in Christ Church on Sunday, November 4, 1739. He was well-received and preached every day that week. On the evening of November 8, Whitefield preached outdoors to an estimated audience of 6,000 listeners, almost half of the city's population.[18] On November 8, both Philadelphia papers noted Whitefield's presence and preaching; Andrew Bradford's *American Weekly Mercury* remarked that Whitefield had arrived and that "People of all Perswasions" were attending his sermons, while Franklin's *Pennsylvania Gazette* included a basic itinerary for the evangelist for the ensuing months. Franklin's report was reprinted by the *Boston Evening-Post* (November 19), the *New England Weekly Journal* (November 20), and the *Boston Weekly News-Letter* (November 22). On November 15, 1739, the *Pennsylvania Gazette* reported that almost 6,000 listeners attended Whitefield's sermon from the Philadelphia Court House steps and "stood in an awful Silence to hear him." The account was reprinted in four of the five Boston papers.[19] Whitefield spent one month preaching in Philadelphia, New York, and the surrounding areas. In that month, seven news items on the evangelist appeared in the Philadelphia papers, and almost three times as many reprints of those articles appeared throughout the colonies, as readers followed news of Whitefield's travels.

The Philadelphia reports represent the majority of news reports on Whitefield during his first preaching tour. Papers highlighted the significant numbers of listeners his preaching drew as well as the attentiveness and receptiveness of audiences. His upcoming itinerary was frequently included as Whitefield's "press agent" William Seward was often responsible for these reports. The high rate of reprinting was also common during Whitefield's first tour and enabled readers in all colonies to keep abreast of Whitefield's ministry.

Along with news reports on the evangelist, contributed letters appeared often in the papers during Whitefield's first tour. Letters were contributed to the papers by readers and offered eye-witness accounts of Whitefield's preaching. Contributors also battled with each other in print over Whitefield, often with one contributor attacking Whitefield or his ministry and another defending him in the next issue. Occasionally, papers would print a contributed poem or excerpt that a reader had culled from a well-known theologian or writer that related to Whitefield or the Awakening. Contributed items such as these accounted for 36 percent of newspaper items on Whitefield during his first tour, with 70 percent of these items being positive toward Whitefield. These items present the public side of Whitefield, lauding his powerful preaching, his impressive effect on the audience, and his apparent godliness. Again, the picture of Whitefield is two-dimensional, with very few contributed letters presenting Whitefield as a true individual or mentioning any personal contact with him.

The letters from Whitefield's second preaching stop in New York are indicative of contributed reader opinion found in the papers during his first tour. Whitefield spent four days preaching in New York City, arriving on Wednesday, November 14, 1739. On November 19, William Bradford's *New-York Gazette* noted his arrival and the masses his preaching drew: "The like Concourse, on such an occasion, was never known here before." The week after Whitefield left the city to return to Philadelphia, the *Gazette* included a three-page anonymous letter regarding the evangelist, including a short biography and an account of Whitefield's preaching in New York:

> I went to hear him in the Evening at the Presbyterian Church, where he Expounded to about 2000 People within and without the Doors. I never in my Life saw so attentive an Audience. Mr. Whitefield spake as one having Authority. All he said was Demonstration, Life and Power! The Peoples Eyes and Ears hung on his Lips. They greedily devour'd every Word. I came home astonished! Every Scruple vanished; I never saw nor heard the like, and I said within my self, *Surely God is with this Man of Truth.* (November 26, 1739)

That same day, John Peter Zenger's *New-York Weekly Journal* printed a poem extolling the evangelist's virtues.

Letters like these tended to reveal both the writer's personal experience with Whitefield and his opinion of Whitefield. As noted above, 70 percent of letters about Whitefield during his first preaching tour were positive toward the evangelist, with contributors lauding Whitefield's preaching, apparent godliness, and power to move audiences. However, negative letters did appear in the papers during the first tour, and Whitefield's stop in New York produced the first significant one. A pamphlet titled "To the Inhabitants of New-York" had appeared on November 17, 1739; it was an open letter to New Yorkers by Anglican clergyman Jonathan Arnold warning readers of tolerating Whitefield, whom Arnold considered "unworthy the Honour of the Gown, or the Character of a Clergyman." Arnold's primary complaint against Whitefield was the evangelist's criticisms of the Church of England. According to his publication, Arnold had met with Whitefield personally and had unsuccessfully attempted to draw him into a debate. Apparently, Whitefield was also displeased with their meeting for on November 27 he wrote from Philadelphia to Philip Bearcroft, secretary of the Society for the Propagation of the Gospel in Foreign Parts, to notify him that he considered Arnold "unworthy of the name of a minister of Jesus Christ."[20]

The New York papers became involved in the debate when the owner of the home in which Whitefield and Arnold met, New York lawyer William Smith,[21] published a rebuttal to Arnold's pamphlet in the *New-York Gazette* on November 26, 1739. During the next two months, Arnold and Whitefield's supporters battled in both the *American Weekly Mercury* in Philadelphia and the *New-York Gazette*, with the *Mercury* publishing seven letters and the *Gazette* printing three, and with each paper reprinting items from the other.[22]

This paper war is representative of most battles over Whitefield in the papers during his first tour. Despite criticism, Whitefield still emerged in the papers as being strongly supported by the majority of readers. Usually, those who wrote against Whitefield were outnumbered. In this battle, Arnold stood alone against William Smith, three writers using pseudonyms, and several anonymous contributors. In addition, Whitefield's supporters during this tour defended the evangelist vigorously. In the New York battle, one anonymous contributor to the *Mercury* offered to "wrestle" in print with Arnold as he attempted to refute Arnold's claims that Whitefield was a charlatan (November 29). William Smith appeared in print to clarify and defend Whitefield's actions on the night of Arnold's visit. Also, in this battle as in others, Whitefield's defenders very quickly turn the attack on the opposers. In this case, Arnold was accused of acting improperly as a minister of God who should have "avoided passing such uncharitable and unjust Censures on his fellow Creatures."[23] He was attacked as an Anglican, the "Bastard Son of such a Church," who needed to "Learn first to mend [his] own loose sinful Life."[24] One contributor even compared Arnold to Sancho Pancho, armor-bearer to Don Quixote, the quintessential example of an earnest, but misguided and laughable, zealot.[25]

Whitefield's popularity during this tour was assured by the significant number of reprints that occurred even with letters related to only local controversies. For example, Bostonians, who had not yet laid eyes on Whitefield, followed the New York dispute through reprints in their own newspapers and even contributed themselves to the defense of the evangelist. The *Boston Weekly Post-Boy* (December 3, 1739), *New England Weekly Journal* (December 4), and *Boston Weekly News-Letter* (December 6) all reprinted William Smith's first response to Arnold in the November 26, 1739, *New-York Gazette*. Interest in the controversy prompted the *Boston Weekly News-Letter* (November 30), *Boston Weekly Post-Boy* (December 3), and *New England Weekly Journal* (December 4) to reprint Arnold's original open letter of November 17, "To the Inhabitants of New-York." Boston publishers Samuel Kneeland and Timothy Green, Jr., made public their dislike of Arnold's attack, noting in their *New England Weekly Journal* that "the Pastors of our Churches have a more grateful Apprehension of the pious & excellent Mr. Whitefield, than to desire any Thing to be Publish'd to his Dishonour, or to hinder the Acceptableness or Success of his Ministry" (December 4). On December 6, anonymous contributor "Philalethes" defended Whitefield in the *Boston Weekly News-Letter*, condemning Arnold's letter as "a Piece wrote with so much Heat and Indiscretion, that has so much Rancour and Scurrility spread over the Face of it, and that so evidently carries its own Confutation along with it."[26]

Unlike Arnold's letter, the vast majority of criticism of Whitefield found in the papers during his first tour reveals that most opponents, like his supporters, viewed Whitefield as more of an image than an individual. After the winter of 1740, which Whitefield spent in the South, opponents in the papers began to respond to him not as just another preacher, but as one who represented a religious movement that was drawing a line in the colonial sand. While the attack by Arnold had been based on a personal encounter with Whitefield, future attacks would not be derived from that type of connection but from the fear of what Whitefield represented in terms of a new direction for colonial Christianity. Whitefield's spirituality included a more engaging, theatrical, emotionally intense style of preaching; a more personal, intimate, relational approach to God; and an emphasis on a New Birth religious experience. The fact that he had followers in the colonies such as revivalists Gilbert Tennent and James Davenport who preached the New Birth as he did made him all the more dangerous.

Specifically, detractors in the papers began to question Whitefield's methods and motives as seen in a controversy Whitefield encountered in Philadelphia after he returned there in April 1740. On May 1, both Franklin's *Pennsylvania Gazette* and Andrew Bradford's *American Weekly Mercury* printed reports on Whitefield's most recent preaching stops throughout the Middle Colonies. Franklin's report ended with an additional paragraph, submitted by William Seward: "Since Mr. Whitefield's Preaching here, the Dancing School, Assembly and Concert Room have been shut up, as inconsistent with the Doctrine of the Gospel: And though the Gentlemen concern'd caus'd the Door to be broke open again, we are inform'd that no Company came the last Assembly Night."[27] The next week, an anonymous letter was published in the *Pennsylvania Gazette* by a defender of the "Persons concerned in the Assembly and Concert," objecting to Seward's suggestion that they did not meet that night because their activities were "inconsistent with the Doctrine of the Gospel." On the contrary, the author claimed, Seward bolted the doors despite being aware that the rooms had been rented for that evening, and the company did not meet on the night in question because it was not their regularly scheduled night. At the close of the letter, the contributor went beyond the incident at hand to question Seward's motives in submitting the news item as he did: "After this Account of Seward's Behaviour, no one can wonder at his low Craft, in getting this Paragraph foisted into the News-Papers just before his Departure for England, in order to carry it along with him, and spread his Master's Fame, as tho' he had met with great Success among the better Sort of People in Pennsylvania, when at the same Time, to his great Mortification, he can't but be sensible that he has been neglected by them." The author also doubted the veracity of Seward's other newspaper reports, asserting that "in all those Articles of News, which give an Account of the vast Crouds who compose his Audience, their Numbers are always exaggerated, being often doubled and sometimes trebled."[28] This questioning of Whitefield's veracity would increase as Whitefield's first preaching tour came to an end.

Detractors also knew enough of the power of celebrity to worry about the public momentum Whitefield was gaining. Letters to the papers during his only preaching stop in Boston reveal concern among opponents of Whitefield that, despite sporadic criticism, he had reached the level of superstardom that placed him out of the reach of critics. Already in the spring of 1740 in Philadelphia, Franklin had acknowledged a concern among readers that Whitefield had secured the press' good favor to such a point that many would not print against him. Before one negative letter printed in his *Pennsylvania Gazette* on May 8, 1740, Franklin noted that he hoped "the publishing of this, will obviate a groundless Report (injurious to that Gentleman) that Mr. Whitefield has engag'd all the Printers not to print any Thing against him." When Whitefield arrived in Boston in September 1740 for a one-month stay in New England, readers had already followed Whitefield's progress through the colonies closely through reprints. Forty percent of all reprints on the Awakening in the colonies appeared in Boston newspapers. The significant amount of reprints in the Boston papers from the *South-Carolina Gazette* and papers in the Middle Colonies certainly influenced how the Boston papers covered Whitefield and his preaching when he arrived there. As in the other colonies, the coverage was frequent and emphasized the number of listeners he drew, audience reactions, and his upcoming itinerary. All five Boston papers noted his arrival in Boston, and close to twenty items on Whitefield appeared in the papers during his one-month stay.

What is notable about Whitefield's time in Boston is an unsuccessful attempt by one newspaper printer to print against the evangelist. On September 29, 1740, Thomas Fleet, printer of the *Boston Evening-Post*, reported the following: "Last Saturday all the Troops raised here for the

Expedition to the West Indies, except Capt. Winslow's Company (who are on board and just upon departing) sail'd from Nantucket for New-York. And this Morning the Rev. Mr. Whitefield set out on his Progress to the Eastward, so that the Town is in a hopeful Way of being restor'd to its former State of Order, Peace and Industry." Three days later on October 2, a contributor to the *Boston Weekly News-Letter* criticized Fleet for insinuating that Whitefield had destroyed the peace of Boston. In his next issue of the *Post* on October 6, Fleet apologized, asserting that he meant to imply that the departure of the troops in the preceding paragraph would allow for order to be reestablished in Boston. Fleet assured his readers that he had never spoken against Whitefield and wished him success in the colonies. One week later, Fleet noted in his *Post* that he had received a contributed letter to publish but could not because "although he [Fleet] is entirely of the ingenious Author's Opinion . . . yet he is obliged to inform him, that he does not think it safe for him to print them at present, having sufficient Proof, that the TRUTH is not to be spoke at all Times."

At this point, Whitefield's support was so strong in the papers that Fleet had to be content with a slightly veiled complaint against White-field's popularity. Four years later, however, Whitefield's status in the papers was weaker, so Fleet could be more direct with his criticism, as a note in his *Post* for December 17, 1744, reveals: "We hear from Cambridge, that the Church and Congregation there have wisely and peaceably agreed not to allow Mr. Whitefield to preach among them; and 'tis believed other Towns will follow this laudable Example."

During his first preaching tour, Whitefield was for many newspaper readers the "experience" of the revival. Readers did not see Whitefield as the leading theologian or pastor of the revival; they saw him as the power of the movement. They went to hear him in order to experience God—to feel the power of God as they shook, cried, and rejoiced. This is the aspect of Whitefield's ministry that comes across most clearly in the papers and is why the charge of "enthusiasm" was leveled so often against him.

His individual "voice" was not present in the newspapers during this preaching tour. Although contributors sometimes directed their queries or concerns to Whitefield himself, the evangelist did not respond personally to any questions or challenges directed to him through the newspapers.[29] Nor did he offer much of his own writing to the papers. Of the thirteen items in the papers authored by Whitefield, it is not clear that any were specifically intended by Whitefield for publication in a newspaper.[30] Besides Jonathan Arnold's report of his time with Whitefield at the beginning of his tour, no personal encounters with the evangelist were reported in the papers. And most news reports focused on the tangibles—number of listeners, amount of money collected, responses of the audience. Very seldom did the papers report even the topics of his sermons. As noted above, contributed letters made up only 36 percent of items printed on Whitefield in the papers during his first preaching tour, so most of what the colonists read during Whitefield's first tour was news, not opinion.

Thus, during his first preaching tour, Whitefield appeared in the papers as an icon that produced for listeners an experience of God. Perhaps one series of letters which appeared in the *South-Carolina Gazette* during the summer of 1740 best exemplifies the iconic status Whitefield experienced in colonial newspapers. On July 12, a letter appeared on the front page of the *South-Carolina Gazette* in which the anonymous author, who identified himself as an Anglican, and whom some scholars suspect to be Anglican Commissary Alexander Garden, used an extended simile to compare Whitefield to a comet:

> You may perhaps have observ'd or heard that when a Comet appears (which you know is a disorderly kind of a Star with a Blaze, that crosses and interferes with the Paths and Motions of the regular Stars, Planets and other heavenly Bodies) what Crowds are collected, and stand whole Mornings and Evenings a Gape, and a Ghast at the new surprizing Sight! What curious Speculations, what witty Remarks, what wise Observations does the new Phantom give rise to? He disdains the lesser Stars around him . . . . And boasting himself in a native and superior Light, bestowed in an extraordinary Manner and Measure, he promises to add fresh Fewel to the Sun, to rekindle his Beams and snuff the Moon. . . . It is highly probable many of those so much reproached regular Stars and Planets, will continue to shine and move on, and to know their appointed Courses and Seasons, when the Comet self-consumed, or attempting to approach too near the Sun shall be exhaled, and vanish like a Vapour; at least in the feeble Eyes of us short sighted Mortals.

The writer's comparison of Whitefield to a comet is indicative of how many viewed him at the time. He was often charged with being "disorderly" and obstructing the efforts of "regular" ministers. He drew crowds of onlookers who were shocked and affected by what they experienced, leading many to "curious Speculations" about the effects of his ministry. Most significantly, Whitefield was often criticized for projecting a sense of superiority, presenting himself as unique among ministers and capable of producing powerful effects by his preaching. This contributor asserts that Whitefield will self-consume, leaving no lasting legacy.

Supporters of Whitefield rallied against the contributor, with one arguing the next week in the *Gazette* that he wished "all our slow and orderly Planets were transform'd into Comets of more Speed and Lustre." Three weeks later on August 8, another opponent claimed Whitefield more resembled "another and more ordinary Phænomenon in Nature, call'd Will with Wisp; which by a strolling kind of Light, seduces People out of the Way, misguides them into Boggs and Fens, and there bewildering leaves them."[31] Comparisons of Whitefield to objects and forces in nature presented him in the papers less as a person and more as an image, a representation of the power and experience of the movement.

Whitefield's Shifting Image: Second Preaching Tour, October 1744-March 1748

Whitefield left the colonies in January 1741, not returning for almost four years. In that time, significant events occurred in the revival movement in America, causing the images of both the revival and Whitefield to shift in the newspapers. Disagreements between those who embraced the New Light and those who did not rose to increasingly acrimonious levels, producing splits in many churches and intense animosity in some churches that held together. The Philadelphia Synod of the Presbyterian church split between Old Side and New Side in May 1741, and the *Pennsylvania Gazette* reported the event in detail on June 11, 1741. The story was reprinted in the *Boston Gazette, Boston Weekly Post-Boy, New England Weekly Journal*, and *South-Carolina Gazette.*[32]

Stories of individual church splits such as the Rev. Samuel Mather's break with the Second Church of Christ in Boston were common, particularly in New England, and followed closely by the papers.[33] Itinerant and lay preaching became a subject of much debate and argument during the years Whitefield was away, as revivalist clergymen such as Gilbert Tennent and James Davenport followed in Whitefield's footsteps and conducted their own itinerant preaching tours. Lay preachers increased throughout the colonies as did unauthorized baptisms and ordinations. Extremism within the revival camp also caused criticism of the movement. When James Davenport led followers in burning religious books in March 1743, the event and its repercussions appeared in the Boston papers for two months and caused extreme embarrassment to revival supporters.[34]

Events such as these led to a change in newspaper reporting on the revival as the papers began to print more negative items. In fact, negative newspaper reports on the revival outnumbered positive ones from 1742 until 1745. Lengthy arguments appeared in the papers as opponents railed against the emotionalism of revival meetings, itinerant and lay preaching, church separations, and the censorious spirit of many revivalists. Official pronouncements against the revival began to be reported by the papers; both Connecticut and New York passed laws regulating activities such as itinerant preaching and the ordination of New Light clergymen.[35] In May 1743, the associated ministers of Boston published a testimony against the Awakening, an act which prompted revival supporters to call for their own testimony in the May 30, 1743, *Boston Weekly Post-Boy*.[36] Five additional letters appeared in the *Boston Gazette* and *Boston Evening-Post* arguing over the meeting and subsequent testimony. In New England, colonists increased their use of the newspapers as vehicles for personal arguments and attacks regarding the Awakening. Connecticut clergyman Andrew Croswell sustained many assaults from revival opponents in the Boston papers and offered his own verbal barbs as well. Massachusetts minister Jonathan Ashley preached against the excesses of the Awakening and was attacked in the *Boston Gazette* by Boston minister William Cooper.[37] Even printers joined in the conflict as the *Boston Evening-Post*'s Thomas Fleet argued with Thomas Prince, Jr., publisher of the revivalist magazine *The Christian History*, over printed criticisms of the revival.[38]

Blame for this religious bickering was often laid at Whitefield's doorstep. One consistent strain throughout the negative letters in the papers is the assertion that the harmful effects of the movement are the fruit of Whitefield's first preaching tour of the colonies. Thus an important shift occurred in Whitefield's persona in the newspapers while he was in England. Just as the newspaper presentation of the revival became more negative, so Whitefield's image shifted from being celebrated as a passionate, holy, powerful representative of the revival to being the originator of the excesses and destructive elements of the movement. Most of this criticism came in the form of contributed letters. During Whitefield's years away from the colonies, ninety-three letters concerning him appeared in the papers. More than 50 percent of the contributed letters were negative—more than twice the amount of negative letters printed during Whitefield's first preaching tour. Criticism of Whitefield was particularly severe in Boston as 30 percent of the letters against Whitefield appeared in the *Boston Evening-Post.*

That Whitefield's image in the papers could so easily shift in his absence is understandable considering the two-dimensional nature of that image. As an icon, he had represented all that was good and hopeful in the movement; now, as the movement was being questioned, Whitefield began to represent everything dangerous or destructive about the revival. Whitefield's revised image had several characteristics. First, his motives became extremely suspect. Contributors began to question Whitefield's goals for his ministry and his financial integrity. Two of the longest series of letters printed in the papers during Whitefield's absence illustrate these concerns. Both series of letters focused on Whitefield's Savannah orphanage Bethesda, the only institutional ministry Whitefield ever sought to build.

The first set of letters originated in Boston and questioned the ministry done at Bethesda. On May 23, 1743, Captain James Hutchinson published a letter in the *Boston Evening-Post* criticizing Bethesda. According to Hutchinson, whom the *Post* noted was "Commander of a Vessel now in this Port," he had visited Bethesda in February and reported that cattle traveled freely through the poorly built edifice and no orphans actually resided there. Hutchinson reported that those living near the orphanage regarded Whitefield "as bad as a Murderer, for enticing poor Orphans to that Place to starve." Three days later on May 26, the *Boston Weekly News-Letter* printed a response, addressed to Thomas Fleet of the *Post*, which questioned some of the facts of Hutchinson's letter. Four days later on May 30, Fleet himself responded in his *Boston Evening-Post* to the "long and puerile Epistle" in the *News-Letter*. Papers in New York and Philadelphia picked up the controversy with reprints of the original letter by Hutchinson in the *Pennsylvania Gazette* (June 2) and the *New-York Weekly Journal* (June 6). On June 9, both the *Pennsylvania Gazette* and the *Pennsylvania Journal* printed a response to Hutchinson from J-----s R----d defending the orphanage and questioning whether Hutchinson had even seen Bethesda.[39] The response was reprinted by the *New-York Weekly Journal* on June 20, while the *Pennsylvania Journal* for June 9 included excerpts from the letter in the May 26 *Boston Weekly News-Letter*. On June 30, the *Pennsylvania Gazette* and the *Pennsylvania Journal* printed a letter from Charleston clergyman Josiah Smith to William Cooper in Boston in which Smith reported that the orphanage was in good condition and was meeting the physical and spiritual needs of many orphans. Smith's letter was reprinted by the *South-Carolina Gazette* on July 4 in a supplement and the *Boston Gazette* on July 5.

The second set of letters began in the *South-Carolina Gazette* and inquired about the financial integrity of Whitefield and his orphanage. On July 4, 1743, the supplement to the *South-Carolina Gazette* contained a letter from "Publicola" which was directed to the managers of Whitefield's orphanage in Savannah. In the absence of Whitefield, the contributor requested that the managers of Bethesda publish information regarding the orphans and employees of the house as well as figures that showed the income of the orphanage and of Whitefield himself.[40] Like the first controversy, papers elsewhere in the colonies reprinted Publicola's July 4 letter.[41] One additional letter from Publicola appeared in the *South-Carolina Gazette* two months before Whitefield arrived for his second preaching tour, and a third letter from Publicola appeared one month after Whitefield had arrived in the colonies in October 1744, garnering various responses from those inside and outside the Whitefield camp.[42] Whitefield himself appeared in the papers on May 22, 1746, printing a summary of his orphanage accounts in the *Pennsylvania Gazette*. The fact that Whitefield felt the need to respond publicly to Publicola in the papers reveals his more defensive position during his second preaching tour.

Another characteristic of Whitefield's revised image is that he was presented in the papers as divisive. The divisiveness of the revival was a major concern for both opponents and supporters of the movement after 1740, and most opponents blamed Whitefield for the censorious, disruptive nature of the movement. On August 30, 1742, a letter against "Whitefieldism" appeared on the front page of the *South-Carolina Gazette*. Twenty sentences long, eighteen of which end with exclamation points, the letter derided Whitefield for causing "Divisions, Strifes, Hatred, and Animosities." In the January 24, 1743, issue of the *Boston Evening-Post*, "Jeremiah Layman" called Whitefield "the first and grand Itinerant," who was to blame for "sowing such Seeds as have taken Root and sprung up, and spread themselves all over the Country in such Fruits, as will destroy the People, if God don't mercifully prevent it." On November 19, 1744, three weeks after Whitefield arrived in the colonies for his second preaching tour, a "Letter from the Country" appeared in the *Boston Evening-Post* blaming Whitefield for the recent "Errors in Doctrine, and gross Disorders in Practice, that have prevail'd so mightily in this Land [and] the many Contentions and Divisions which have disturbed and broken up so many of our Churches." This new aspect of Whitefield's image in the newspapers is quite a departure from the man who initially appeared as one who could unite the many Christian persuasions in the colonies through his emphasis on the fundamentals of the New Birth.

The fruit of Whitefield's two-dimensional, iconic persona in the papers during his first tour is revealed most clearly in the final characteristic of his new image—genuine confusion or disagreement over the real George Whitefield. The lack of an intimate, personal element in Whitefield's first image in the papers perhaps led to this disagreement. During Whitefield's absence from the colonies, he was given many labels by his opposers. The letter on "Whitefieldism" in the August 30, 1742, *South-Carolina Gazette* obviously presented Whitefield as representing a movement rather than as an individual, as the title reveals. Yet the author cannot decide if Whitefield is truly a "Moravian," a "firebrand Enthusiast," or a "Popish Emissary."[43] The *Boston Evening-Post* for May 30, 1743, printed a letter from a contributor in South Carolina to a friend in Glasgow, Scotland, that described Whitefield as a hypocrite: "No Man ever had greater Pretensions to true Religion and Piety. No Man ever possessed a less true-like Christian Spirit." The author also identified Whitefield as a "Popish Emissary." These new labels of Moravian, Enthusiast, Catholic secret agent, and hypocrite would trouble Whitefield throughout his second preaching tour and reflect a shift in his image in the papers.

Whitefield's contributions to the colonial newspapers during his absence from the American colonies reveal an awareness of his shifting image. Whether Whitefield himself offered these letters to the papers or whether they were contributed by his supporters, the letters are different than Whitefield's communications in the papers during his first preaching tour. They are more personal and offer readers details about Whitefield's ministry in what can be interpreted as an attempt to defend aspects of his ministry. On March 16, 1742, the *Boston Gazette* printed a letter from Whitefield to the students at Harvard and Yale in which the evangelist expressed his satisfaction at hearing that many students were becoming "warmed with the Love of God." Whitefield had criticized the spiritual climate of Harvard in his early journals.[44] On April 5, 1742, the *Boston Weekly Post-Boy* printed Whitefield's response to a gentleman in Boston who had questioned the existence of Whitefield's Savannah orphanage. On May 24, 1743, the *Boston Gazette* printed a letter from Whitefield to a Rev. Willison which explained Whitefield's reception by the Associate Presbytery in Scotland and detailed Whitefield's belief in ecumenicalism in all but "Fundamentals" and his adherence to the Westminster Confession of Faith and the articles of the Church of England.

By the time Whitefield arrived for his second preaching tour of the colonies in October 1744, the newspapers had greatly curtailed their coverage of the evangelist. Only eleven items relating to Whitefield appeared in the papers in 1744 before Whitefield arrived. However, once Whitefield arrived in the colonies, papers increased their coverage, with twenty-one items appearing on Whitefield during the two months after he arrived. While only 113 items appeared on the Awakening in general during 1744, almost 200 items were printed in the papers during 1745.

Whitefield's image in the papers was different during his second preaching tour. As noted above, Whitefield had been blamed for impure motives and divisiveness during his time away from the colonies, and his contributions to the colonial papers had become more personal and more defensive. Whitefield's image in the papers during his second preaching tour was much more nuanced and less iconic than his image during his first preaching tour. Several new characteristics of Whitefield's image in the papers during his second tour can be noted.

First, Whitefield's opponents no longer simply questioned his motives and results; they labeled him as downright dangerous to the welfare of colonial Christianity and society. They began their warnings early, with one contributor to the *Boston Evening-Post* for October 29, 1744, asserting that "the sincere lovers of the Peace, Order and Safety of our Churches, have Reason to deprecate his coming; especially considering that he has been the instrumental Cause of those Divisions and Contentions which have rent to Pieces so many Churches in this and the neighboring Governments; and that it is more than probable he will come in the same Spirit, and prosecute the same Design." As noted above, a letter in the November 19 *Boston Evening-Post* blamed Whitefield for the "many Contentions and Divisions which have disturbed and broken up so many of our Churches."[45] The contributor warned readers against accepting Whitefield into their pulpits. Both the *American Weekly Mercury* (December 6) and the *South-Carolina Gazette* (February 4, 1745) reprinted the letter. On November 12, the *South-Carolina Gazette* featured a poem criticizing what the poet called the late "Whitefieldian Farce." On January 28, 1745, the *Boston Evening-Post* published a table noting which Boston ministers had invited Whitefield to preach in their churches and which had not. In other issues of the *Post* and *Boston Weekly News-Letter*, the decisions by the Revs. Nathaniel Appleton, Nathaniel Eells, and Nathaniel Henchman to refuse Whitefield their pulpits were detailed.[46]

Another new characteristic of Whitefield's image in the papers was its lack of uniformity throughout the colonies. During his first preaching tour, Whitefield's image had been consistent in papers in the South,

Middle Colonies, and New England. With his second preaching tour, Whitefield's image began to take on different emphases in different regions of the colonies. In New England, the divisiveness of his earlier ministry was heavily emphasized in the papers. New England particularly had experienced troubling splits in churches during Whitefield's absence as revival supporters left their Old Light pastors and established new congregations. Connecticut and Massachusetts had suffered thirty-two church splits between 1742 and 1745,[47] so it is not surprising that comments against Whitefield's divisiveness were especially strong in New England. The presence of Thomas Fleet, printer of the *Boston Evening-Post*, also affected Whitefield's image in the Boston papers. Of the eighty-five negative letters that were printed in the colonial papers about Whitefield during his second preaching tour, fifty-three were printed in Fleet's *Boston Evening-Post*. Not surprisingly, Whitefield's supporters in Boston made concerted efforts to present him in the papers as being against church divisions. Comments like the following in the *Boston Gazette* for August 20, 1745, appeared frequently in reports of Whitefield's preaching: "Every where the Congregations were very large, and he [Whitefield] was very explicit against the Separations and some erroneous wild Notions which were propagating in those Parts."

Whitefield was still quite popular in the Middle Colonies, especially Philadelphia, and his image in the papers did not suffer there as much as it did in New England. For example, when Whitefield arrived for the second time in Philadelphia in May 1746, Franklin printed Whitefield's financial accounts for his orphanage in his May 22, 1746, *Pennsylvania Gazette* in order to quell criticisms of improper fiscal dealings by the evangelist. The *Pennsylvania Journal* printed weekly updates on Whitefield's preaching stops and often noted the large crowds present to hear him. On July 25, 1746, the *Journal* printed a lengthy appreciation of Whitefield, perhaps written by Benjamin Franklin, which extolled the evangelist and his ministry. The encomium was reprinted in the *Pennsylvania Gazette, New-York Weekly Post-Boy, Boston Gazette*, and *South-Carolina Gazette*.[48] One month later, Whitefield preached a sermon celebrating the victory of the colonial military forces over the French in Louisburg, Nova Scotia. Franklin praised Whitefield's sermon in his paper on August 28, 1746. Upon Whitefield's departure from Philadelphia, Franklin noted in his September 25, 1746, *Gazette* that Whitefield "never was so generally well esteemed by Persons of all Ranks among us." Letters of praise for Whitefield from Philadelphia were printed in papers in Boston, New York, and Charleston.[49] He was similarly supported in the South; for example, the *South-Carolina Gazette* for December 8, 1746, printed a letter from a writer in Philadelphia to a recipient in Boston that compared Whitefield to the great Greek orator Demosthenes.

Despite continued support in the Middle Colonies and the South, Whitefield's character in the papers was increasingly vulnerable during his second preaching tour, evidenced by the sheer number and intensity of the competing images presented by contributors. Many letters to the papers from Whitefield's opponents have his character as their primary focus and many are notable for their passion. The *Virginia Gazette* for October 31, 1745, accused Whitefield of seeking "carnal Self-Interest and Applause," while he was charged with breaking his ordination vows by "praying extempore, and changing the Order of Words to those of his own Fancy" in the *American Weekly Mercury* (February 29, 1746). Letters in the *Boston Evening-Post* judged him proud and self-aggrandizing (August 4 and August 18, 1746), while another contributor to the *Post* charged him with driving "sober and judicious" colonial dissenters to Anglicanism (January 19, 1747). In the February 4, 1745, issue of the *Boston Evening-Post*, "Rusticus" addressed the Boston ministers who supported Whitefield, asking them why they "shou'd set on going again that Engine of Enthusiasm and Error, who did so much Mischief (if setting this whole Land together by the Ears, in quarrellings and Disputes, and dividing of Families and Churches, and in setting People against their Pastors and Teachers, may be call'd so) among us about four Years ago." The Rev. Nathaniel Eells of Norwell, Massachusetts, even balked at attributing any principal part of the New England revival to Whitefield.[50]

Yet his supporters used the papers to present a different Whitefield. The Rev. William Shurtleff of Portsmouth, New Hampshire, remarked, "Every Time I see him, I find my Heart further drawn out towards him" in a *South-Carolina Gazette* reprint from the *Christian History* (February 11, 1745). A contributor calling himself "Nicholas Nameless" in the *Virginia Gazette* for October 31, 1745, reported that the only sound that interrupted Whitefield's preaching in Hanover, Virginia, was "every now and then a Groan or Sob from his Hearers." In a letter to a friend in Boston, Josiah Smith of South Carolina reported that Whitefield was viewed as "the Wonder of the Age" in Charleston.[51] An exceptional "Christian Orator," a contributor to the *South-Carolina Gazette* dubbed him on December 8, 1746.

The victor in the battle over Whitefield's image in the papers during his second preaching tour might have been his supporters because Whitefield continued to draw large crowds throughout his visit to the colonies. His farewell sermon in Boston was reported in the *Pennsylvania Gazette* on September 3, 1748, as drawing 20,000 listeners. Yet Whitefield's image had shifted during the 1740s from that of an icon representing the power of a movement to one that was more nuanced, more controversial, and more vulnerable to criticism. Whitefield would continue to work to manage his image throughout his years as an itinerant evangelist in all the places in which he preached.

GILBERT TENNENT

Although Whitefield certainly appeared more often in colonial newspapers than did any other revivalist during the religious events of the 1740s, his absence from America from January 1741 until October 1744 provided opportunities for local revivalists to receive newspaper coverage. South Carolina planter Hugh Bryan and his ecstatic prophecies appeared in the *South-Carolina Gazette* (March 6, 1742), Connecticut minister Andrew Croswell conducted his own preaching tours and attacked revival moderates in the *Boston Weekly Post-Boy* (April 12, 1742), New England clergymen John Caldwell and John Moorhead battled over doctrine in both the *Boston Gazette* (December 7, 1742) and *Boston Evening-Post* (January 3, 1743), and the travels and alleged infractions of New England itinerants Samuel Buell and Daniel and Nathaniel Rogers were reported tirelessly by the *Boston Evening-Post* (e. g., May 3, 1742; December 12, 1743). Yet, only two American revivalists received newspaper coverage that was, for short periods, comparable to that of Whitefield. For a time, both Gilbert Tennent and James Davenport appeared frequently in colonial newspapers and, like Whitefield, struggled to deal with the shifting personas the papers presented.

Gilbert Tennent's beginnings were quite different from Whitefield's. Born in Ireland to clergyman William Tennent, Sr., and his wife Katherine, Gilbert was the eldest of four sons. His father served as his spiritual director and educator and was very influential in Gilbert's early life. William emphasized internal spirituality over external church participation, contended that conviction of sin must precede true repentance, and looked to God rather than human reason to impart saving knowledge. These convictions led William to renounce his ordination in the Church of Ireland in 1718, and the family immigrated to Philadelphia. Ordained in the Presbyterian denomination in the colonies, William founded a seminary called the Log College in Warminster, Pennsylvania, which produced young ministers with similar convictions. Gilbert's later accounts record his personal spiritual struggles until his conversion in 1723. Because of the instruction he received from his father, Gilbert was awarded the M. A. from Yale College in 1725 and was licensed by the Philadelphia Presbytery that May. He was ordained in New Brunswick, New Jersey, in 1726, having been invited by the inhabitants to organize a Presbyterian church.

Gilbert Tennent's ministry in New Brunswick brought a second significant influence into his life—the ministry and teachings of Dutch Reformed pastor Theodore Frelinghuysen. The only other minister in the immediate vicinity, Frelinghuysen taught the accepted pietist understanding that three steps were necessary for true conversion: a recognition of and struggle with sin, a rebirth by reception of the Holy Spirit, and the subsequent practice of personal piety. A minister's primary duty was to determine his parishioners' spiritual conditions and encourage them toward spiritual rebirth. Ministerial fraternity was determined not by denominational affinity but by clergymen's personal experience with conversion and faithfulness to Reformed theology and practical piety. These convictions soon became Tennent's own, and he became well-known in Presbyterian circles during the 1730s for his revivalist preaching and his strong support of examinations of ministerial candidates for evidence of true conversion.[52]

Tennent met Whitefield in November 1739 soon after the English evangelist arrived for his first preaching tour of the colonies. The men shared similar evangelical leanings, and Whitefield was impressed with Tennent, recording in his journal: "I went to the meeting-house to hear

Mr. Gilbert Tennent preach, and never before heard such a searching sermon. He convinced me more and more that we can preach the Gospel of Christ no further than we have experienced the power of it in our own hearts. . . . Hypocrites must either soon be converted or enraged at his preaching. He is a son of thunder, and does not fear the faces of men" (347-48). The men became friends and allies, and Tennent accompanied Whitefield for several days on the evangelist's tour through New York and New Jersey, introducing him to important revivalist preachers in the area. Whitefield soon left the Middle Colonies for the South, but contact with Whitefield encouraged Tennent in his ministry as a revivalist.

On March 8, 1740, three months after Whitefield's departure, Tennent preached what became the most famous, or infamous, sermon of the revival. The Presbyterian church in Nottingham, Pennsylvania, was searching for a new minister, and both revival supporters and opponents were seeking the pulpit. Called in by revivalists to convince the congregation to choose a New Light pastor, Tennent preached *The Danger of an Unconverted Ministry*. The sermon was a scathing attack on unconverted ministers: "The Ministry of natural [unconverted] Men, is for the most part unprofitable. . . . Is a blind Man fit to be a Guide in a very dangerous Way? Is a dead Man fit to bring others to Life?"[53] Tennent ended the sermon with the suggestion that the dangers of ministry by unconverted clergymen made it "both lawful and expedient to go from them to hear Godly Persons."[54] Not surprisingly, the sermon caused much disturbance, not only among local Presbyterians, but throughout the colonies, as the sermon was printed later that year in Philadelphia and in 1742 in Boston. Tennent was branded a religious enthusiast and his encouragement of leaving "unconverted" ministers turned many against him.

Tennent's Nottingham sermon was not noted by colonial newspapers, but later contributors to the papers referenced the sermon for years to come as an example of Tennent's censorious nature.[55] After Tennent's first wife passed away in the summer of 1740, he began to minister as an itinerant preacher. He made a short preaching tour through southern New Jersey, Delaware, and northern Maryland, again not appearing in the newspapers. In November 1740, Tennent received another visit from Whitefield in his New Brunswick home.

Whitefield had just returned to the Middle Colonies from a preaching tour of New England, and he convinced Tennent to follow in his footsteps. Daniel Rogers, then a young Harvard tutor and later himself an itinerant preacher, was to accompany Tennent to Boston. The pair left New Brunswick on the eve of the coldest winter New England had seen in thirty years. Tennent preached through Long Island and Rhode Island on his way to Boston, arriving in the city on December 13, 1740. He preached in Boston and nearby towns and continued up to York, Maine, making numerous stops along the way. Passing through Boston again briefly, Tennent preached through southeastern Massachusetts and along the coastal towns of Rhode Island and Connecticut on his way home to New Brunswick.[56]

Tennent's 1740-1741 New England preaching tour marked the clergyman's emergence as a significant figure in colonial newspaper coverage of the religious events of the 1740s.[57] Next to Whitefield, Tennent appeared in the papers more than did any other clergyman, and, with James Davenport, is the only other colonial revivalist to achieve intercolonial notice, as reports of his actions appeared in the papers as far away as South Carolina.[58] His time in the papers was shorter-lived and more localized than was Whitefield's, peaking during the years 1741-1743. The majority of the items on Tennent were printed in papers in Boston and Philadelphia, with seven items appearing in the *South-Carolina Gazette*.[59]

Although his time in the spotlight was shorter, Tennent's persona in the colonial newspapers shifted during the years of the Awakening just as Whitefield's had done. However, the reasons for Tennent's shift were different from Whitefield's, just as Tennent's persona in the colonial newspapers was different from Whitefield's. An examination of newspaper coverage of Tennent's New England tour reveals the disparities.

Tennent's New England Preaching Tour: 1740-1741

In some ways, Tennent's persona in the colonial newspapers during his New England tour was similar to Whitefield's during the English evangelist's 1739-1741 preaching tour of the colonies. Like Whitefield, Tennent was given close coverage, particularly by the Boston papers.

Almost 30 percent of all the newspaper items on Tennent that were printed in the papers during 1739-1748 appeared during his New England tour, as Figure 3.3 reveals. When one includes reprints, a total of thirteen news items, five letters, and three poems were printed regarding Tennent's New England tour.

News reports on the tour were similar to Whitefield's in that they typically offered information on Tennent's preaching schedule and extolled his preaching and popularity as well as his positive reception by listeners. All the news items printed on Tennent's tour presented the revivalist in a positive light. Typical is a report by the *New England Weekly Journal* for December 23, 1741, which noted Tennent's preaching stops and the popularity of his preaching at the Rev. Benjamin Colman's church "where was a vast crowded Assembly, & several Hundreds were forc'd to go away not being able to get into the House." On April 7, the *Journal* described his farewell sermon in New London with a similarly positive tone: "He address'd the Auditories from Time to Time in so pathetic & fervent a manner, that it seemed to give the most stout & obdurate Transgressors, sensible & deep Compunction of Soul." News reports were reprinted by the *Pennsylvania Gazette* in Philadelphia and the *South-Carolina Gazette* in Charleston.[60]

Like the news reports, the letters and poems contributed to the papers were similarly positive regarding Tennent. On January 27, 1742, the *New England Weekly Journal* carried a letter from a contributor in Portsmouth, New Hampshire, which praised Tennent's preaching: "none that heard his Sermons here, more especially the two last, can open their Lips to the Disparagement of the sacred Performances." Another letter in the *Journal* for March 24 from a clergyman complimented Tennent's hellfire-and-brimstone preaching as deserving to be "applauded and imitated." On June 18, the *South-Carolina Gazette* printed a letter from Rhode Island to a recipient in Charlestown, Massachusetts, describing Tennent's activities: "His Endeavours to make Proselytes has been indefatigable, having preached every Day in the Week to a crowded Audience Three Times a Day." Three poems appeared in the Boston newspapers in March 1741 praising Tennent's ministry. One, printed in the *Boston Weekly News-Letter* on March 5, encouraged Tennent in his future ministry: "Go, blessed Boanerges, go / Let Sinners hear / That Wrath is near / And urge to shun th' impending

Blow / Excite the wounded Soul to fly to Christ / As he alone can heal and give it Rest."[61] On March 17, a poem in the *New England Weekly Journal* ended with a prayer for Tennent's safety against all foes: "Let Angel Bind, dear Tennent's Guards appear, / And strike his Foes with Blindness or with Fear. / O now bless'd Champion, let they Courage raise, / Thou'rt safe in Christ, tho' many Hells should blaze."[62]

Also like Whitefield, Tennent encountered his share of criticism, although again, like Whitefield's first visit, opponents were in the minority during Tennent's New England tour. One contributor to the *South-Carolina Gazette* for June 18, 1741, offered extracts of several letters from New England condemning Tennent as "a Person worthy of his [Whitefield's] Recommendation, with every thing rude, vulgar, and uncouth in Person, Doctrine and Expression, whom a great part of the Town have rambled after all this Winter in dreadful Cold and Snow, whereby Multitudes of all Sexes and Ages are bro't under Conviction and real Distraction." One writer in Charlestown, Massachusetts, complained that during Tennent's sermons, a listener might hear himself "cursed, damned, double-damned, the Generality stiled unregenerate, proud, Hypocrites, rotten-hearted, old Sinners, and Devils, and worse than Devils." The last letter, from Connecticut to a recipient in Boston, reported that Tennent preached with such "dolorous and frightful Images, that he has scared half the People, especially Women and Children, almost out of their Wits." As these excerpts show, like Whitefield, Tennent was criticized for actions which many identified with unhealthy religious enthusiasm such as extemporaneous, emotional preaching. Also like Whitefield, Tennent was criticized for promulgating the evangelical doctrines of original sin and the need for repentance for true Christian conversion. However, these critics were in the vast minority during Tennent's New England preaching tour.

Thus, in some ways, Tennent appeared in the papers during his tour as Whitefield initially did—popular, effective, a messenger of God. However, also like Whitefield, Tennent's persona in the papers eventually shifted, but for different reasons. The disparity can be found in how each man approached his relationship with the colonial newspapers. Whitefield, as noted above, allowed himself to be presented as an icon in the papers, revealing very little of himself personally. His contributions to the newspapers tended to be reports on his preaching travels or excerpts from his journals. Very seldom did he re-spond publicly to letters addressed to him in the papers, and he did not print letters dealing with personal matters. Tennent, on the other hand, was willing to respond personally to letters addressed to him in the pa-pers and also experienced publication of his personal views and doubts. These differences account for the varying shifts each man experienced in terms of his representation in the papers.

Tennent's willingness to personally address critics is revealed in his response to the single negative letter that appeared in the Boston papers during his New England tour. On January 12, 1741, the *Boston Weekly Post-Boy* printed a letter addressed to Tennent that questioned the revivalist's motives for leaving his own congregation to preach throughout New England. Tennent responded two weeks later in the *New England Weekly Journal* for January 27 from a preaching stop in Marblehead, on the coast of Massachusetts. In his response, Tennent noted that his own church was supplied with neighboring ministers and that his preaching in New England had produced good results: "For in divers Places, which I have been in, since I left home, that good God (who will not Seal a Blank) has graciously visibly and uncommonly bless'd my poor Labours to the spiritual Good of many Souls. . . . In extraordinary Times, when the Spirit of God is uncommonly poured forth, may not extraordinary Methods be pursu'd, without Censure?" This type of self-defense had never appeared in the papers from Whitefield's pen and would only increase from Tennent in the months following his tour. Tennent's letter reveals a willingness on his part to address critics directly and personally.

Public Doubts: The Aftermath of the New England Preaching Tour

Tennent's persona in the newspapers shifted dramatically after his New England preaching tour. Tennent's personal contributions to the newspapers, which increased significantly after the tour, can be seen as being for the most part responsible for the shift. During 1742 and 1743, 70 percent of all letters by or about Tennent printed in the papers during the revival appeared. [63] According to Tennent's biographer Mil-ton J. Coalter, Jr., Tennent experienced several incidents in the months following his tour that played a significant role in causing him to reassess the goals and practices of the revival.[64] Beginning in the spring of 1742, one year after the end of his New England tour, these doubts and concerns were played out in the newspapers and produced harsh and accusatory responses. Tennent's persona in the papers began to shift from being a celebrated revivalist preacher in the vein of Whitefield, to being defensive, embattled, and uncertain.

The events that brought concern to Tennent began in June of 1741 when the Philadelphia Synod of the Presbyterian denomination split over conflict about the revival and the related issue of improper ordination to the ministry. The pro-revival clergymen, with Tennent among them, formed their own synod. The *Pennsylvania Gazette* reported the split on June 11, 1741, also noting that Tennent had preached in the new building in Philadelphia that had been constructed for Whitefield.[65] The *Gazette* report was reprinted by the *Boston Gazette* (June 22), *Boston Weekly Post-Boy* (June 22), *New England Weekly Journal* (June 23), and *South-Carolina Gazette* (July 23).

Also distressing to Tennent was the increase in traveling preachers, particularly in New England, both ordained and lay, who took Tennent's attacks on the New England clergy as validation for their "unauthorized" preaching in established parishes. James Davenport, the best known of the traveling exhorters, preached throughout Connecticut and Rhode Island in the summer of 1741, naming "unconverted" ministers from the pulpit and leading his followers in singing hymns in the streets. The papers reported readers' consternation over the itinerants: "We hear from the Eastward, that many Towns there are in violent Commotions, occasioned by the extraordinary Conduct of some itinerant [sic] Preachers they have had among 'em."[66]

Lastly, in November 1741, Tennent met briefly in New York City with the leader of the Moravian movement, the German nobleman Count Nicholas Ludwig von Zinzendorf. At the time, the pietistic Moravians were working to establish a settlement in Pennsylvania, but their beliefs in salvation by human free will and perfectionism, the ability of the regenerate to reach a state of sinless perfection while still on earth, had already caused conflict with other revivalists such as Whitefield. Tennent also disliked their principles and began to fear that unconventional beliefs and practices such as theirs would be a product of the excesses of the revival.[67]

Again, Tennent showed his willingness to respond to these incidents through the public prints. He responded to the Presbyterian split with his *Remarks upon a Protestation Presented to the Synod of Philadelphia, June 1, 1741* (Philadelphia, 1741). Tenennt expressed his concerns about Count Zinzendorf and the Moravians in his *Necessity of Holding Fast the Truth*, to which was appendixed *Some Account of the Principles of the Moravians*, which was published in early 1743 (Boston: S. Kneeland and T. Green, 1743).

Tennent's apprehensions also appeared in the newspapers, revealed to the public in several printed letters. These letters indicate Tennent's anxiety over the direction the revival was taking. In the spring of 1742, a few months after meeting with Zinzendorff, a letter from Tennent to a minister in Connecticut appeared in the *Boston Weekly News-Letter* on April 15. In the letter, Tennent responded to correspondence he had received from New England regarding his preaching tour one year earlier. Tennent's letter contained a warning against encouraging lay exhorting which could lead to "the grossest Errors and the greatest Anarchy and Confusion." Also in the letter was a denunciation of the Moravians, whose doctrines Tennent criticized as a "confused Medly of rank Antinomianism and Quakerism." Tennent also worried that "the Churches in America, and elsewhere, are in great hazard of Enthusiasm." The letter was reprinted by the *Boston Evening-Post* on May 3. A second item by Tennent appeared one month later on May 11 in the *Boston Gazette*, probably an excerpt from Tennent's *Some Account of the Principles of the Moravians*. The excerpt warns readers to beware of the Moravians whom Tennent believes are departing from biblical Christianity. The excerpt was reprinted by the *Boston Weekly News-Letter* on May 13.

According to the papers, both of these items were sent by Tennent to the contributors, although it is not known if Tennent desired them to be published in the papers. They reveal Tennent's willingness to address the concerns of the movement, as well as Tennent's personal style of criticism. Tennent's letters to the papers, unlike Whitefield's, tended to use extreme language and to preclude the possibility of a middle road. As Tennent's April 15 letter shows, phrases such as "grossest Errors," "greatest Anarchy and Confusion," "rank Antinomianism," and "in great hazard of Enthusiasm" when condemning lay preaching and the

Moravians reveal his tendency to demonize those he did not agree with and draw battle lines that were difficult to cross. As a "son of thunder," Tennent's style of public argument may have in part been responsible for the vehemence of the attacks that soon came against him.

These counterattacks were sparked two months later on July 22, 1742, by a letter from Tennent published in the *Boston Weekly News-Letter*. An excerpt from a letter Tennent had written to moderate revivalist John Dickinson of New Jersey, the letter was contributed by revival foe Thomas Clap, President of Yale College, who claimed to have the original in his possession. In the letter, Tennent discussed the split in the Philadelphia Synod and the current revivalist practices of holding separate meetings, judging the spiritual states of others, singing in public, and encouraging lay preaching, noting revivalist James Davenport as one of the chief propagators. This letter revealed the two aspects of Tennent's contributions to the papers that were becoming standard—his extreme, divisive language and his openness and frankness with his personal thoughts and feelings.

In the letter, Tennent expressed concern about the "Danger of every Thing which tends to Enthusiasm and Division in the visible Church." Tennent condemned the practice of judging the spiritual states of others as "inscriptural," "Schismatical," and "of awful Tendency to rend and tear the Church." Holding separate revivalist meetings is "enthusiastical, proud, and schismatical"; naming ministers as unconverted is a "pernicious Practice"; encouraging lay preaching is a "most perverse Practice"; and singing in public is "enthusiastical Ostentation." He believed such "enthusiastical Fooleries" represented "much Mischief to the poor Church of God." Tennent also declared his "Abhorrence" of all encouragement of immediate, personal revelation. Noteworthy in Tennent's condemnation of these practices is not only the fact that he himself had formerly promoted and performed such actions, but also his strong language of denunciation.

Tennent also evidenced in this letter his characteristic openness about his personal thoughts. In referencing the synod split, Tennent criticized his own "excessive heat of Temper." He also remarked that since his New England preaching tour, he had been "visited with much spiritual Desertions, Temptations, and Distresses of various kinds . . . which have given me a greater Discovery of myself, then I think I ever had before." Although it appears that Tennent did not plan for the letter to be publicized, the revelation of his personal doubts about his role in the Awakening caused his image in the papers to be quickly attacked. The letter was widely reprinted, appearing in the *Boston Evening-Post* (July 26, 1742), *American Weekly Mercury* (August 12), *Pennsylvania Gazette* (August 12), and *South-Carolina Gazette* (December 6).

Tennent's letter produced immediate responses from both pro- and anti-revivalists. Taking exception with Tennent's condemnation of lay preaching, one contributor to the August 26 issue of the *American Weekly Mercury* in Philadelphia, possibly a Quaker, defended lay preaching with an excerpt from *A Defence of Primitive Christianity* by John Trenchard and Thomas Gordon (London, 1720-1721). Revivalist opponent Rev. David Evans, a pastor in Piles Grove, New Jersey, who had been dismissed from his congregation in 1740 because of his opposition to the revival, printed a lengthy letter in the September 2, 1742, *Pennsylvania Gazette* in which he attempted to show how Tennent and the other revivalists, particularly Whitefield, had committed exactly the acts Tennent condemned in his letter to Dickinson. Evans' letter was reprinted in the *South-Carolina Gazette* on March 14, 1743.

Unlike Whitefield, Tennent had allowed his personal feelings about the religious events of the day to become public knowledge, and his questioning of practices he had formerly advocated placed him in a position to be attacked and criticized. Again, Tennent showed a willingness to engage in debate with newspaper readers, publishing a response on September 2, 1742, in the same issue of the *Pennsylvania Gazette* in which Evans' letter appeared. Tennent attempted to clarify his earlier letter to Dickinson, which he noted was published without his knowledge or consent. He claimed he never believed "the Matter or Substance" of his contentions with the Philadelphia Synod were wrong, that he does not question James Davenport's "Piety and Integrity," and that parishioners should not "sit contentedly under" a minister who attempts to hinder the progress of the Awakening. Tennent acknowledged that unconverted ministers can have useful labors, and he again discouraged naming ministers as unconverted, allowing lay preachers, singing in public streets, and following emotional impulses instead of the Bible.

Tennent's explanatory letter of September 2 did nothing to stem the tide of criticism against him. In fact, it may have provoked even more. On October 21, 1742, "Philanthropos" appeared in the *Pennsylvania Gazette* in response to both of Tennent's letters, accusing Tennent of attempting to distance himself from the revival he helped create. Six weeks later on December 8, two ministers continued the debate in the postscript of the *Pennsylvania Gazette*. David Evans contributed again, carefully dissecting Tennent's second letter to show how Tennent had committed the very acts he spoke against in his letter. In a long letter, Samuel Finley, ordained as a Presbyterian evangelist in October 1742 and later pastor of a church in Nottingham, Pennsylvania, defended Tennent against the accusations by Philanthropos by claiming that from the outset of the revival, Tennent and the other revivalists consistently spoke against irregularities such as outcries and always affirmed an orthodox understanding of salvation. In Boston, Tennent's letter of clarification was reprinted from the September 2, 1742, *Pennsylvania Gazette* by the *Boston Weekly News-Letter* (September 23) and the *Boston Evening-Post* (September 27), with the *Post* also reprinting David Evans' first letter in its October 11 issue and reprinting Philanthropos' letter from the October 21 *Pennsylvania Gazette* in its November 8 issue. Two additional responses against Tennent appeared within a week of each other in Boston.[68]

The response to Tennent's public misgivings about the revival continued through the first few months of 1743, with letters appearing in the *Boston Evening-Post* (January 17), *New-York Weekly Post-Boy* (February 1), and *Boston Weekly News-Letter* (February 17). Tennent was also mentioned throughout the spring in letters that insisted that the revival had reached its end.[69] Similar to the newspaper criticisms was an anonymous publication by John Hancock of Boston that appeared in the winter of 1743 titled *The Examiner; Or Gilbert against Tennent* (Boston). At one point using a two-column format to make his point, Hancock showed how Tennent's criticisms against the Moravians in *The Necessity of Holding Fast the Truth* directly contradicted his assertions in his sermon *The Danger of an Unconverted Ministry*.

The response to Tennent's doubts about the revival reveal how far Tennent's persona in the newspapers had moved from being celebrated as a revivalist in the manner of Whitefield. Instead of representing the power and potential of the movement as Whitefield had, Tennent began to represent the mistakes and self-doubt of the revival. Certainly being local made Tennent a much easier target for criticism from colonial readers. He could not escape across the ocean as could Whitefield. Tennent's tendencies to use extreme, polarizing language also fueled criticism against him. And his willingness to debate publicly with his critics made him appear more human and vulnerable than a revivalist such as Whitefield.

The motives behind Tennent's willingness to debate publicly may have stemmed from naiveté. Certainly he did not manage his public image as well as did Whitefield. His shift from iconic revivalist to uncertain individual was rapid and caused primarily by his openness to the public. Yet, perhaps it is more accurate to regard the difference in the two men as stemming from how they viewed themselves and their ministries. Whitefield consistently presented himself as a preacher and evangelist, viewing his ministry as one of conversion, not discipleship. He had no consistent parish throughout his lifetime and did not write works of theology. Tennent, on the other hand, perhaps viewed himself more as a pastor. Throughout his life, he appeared concerned for the overall spiritual growth and maturity of his parishioners. Tennent's biographer Milton J. Coalter, Jr. argues that Tennent's Nottingham sermon was an attempt to jar his Presbyterian colleagues out of their lifeless religious formalism by emphasizing religion of the heart, while his criticisms of the Moravians was an effort to stifle the equally erroneous move to the extreme of religious emotionalism. Coalter also notes that Tennent spent the later years of his ministry working not for conversion but for education, attempting to give his parishioners a solid foundation in Christian doctrine in order to strengthen their faith.[70] Perhaps this pastoral tendency made Tennent unable to resist attempting to correct the errors of the movement and to defend what he saw as benefits of the new direction of colonial Christianity. Certainly Tennent was unwilling to allow the errors of the revival to continue undenounced. He was also prepared to criticize other ministers he believed were hurting the revival, and he wrote many theological works attempting to correct mistakes in the movement. Thus, Tennent's more consistent and more open engagement with the religious events of the time made him more susceptible to criticism and made his public image in the papers more vulnerable to shifts and attack.

Tennent continued to write in an attempt to defend and redirect the movement, publishing *The Examiner, Examined; Or Gilbert Tennent, Harmonious* (Philadelphia, 1743) in response to Hancock. He also appeared in the *Pennsylvania Gazette* on June 30, 1743, and July 7, 1743, in attempts to counter answers from Count Zinzendorf published in the *Gazette* on May 19 regarding theological doctrines such as the New Birth and justification by faith. Tennent decided in the fall of 1743 to leave his New Brunswick church and pastor the congregation of the New Building in Philadelphia. The report of the move by the *Boston Evening-Post* on November 14 reveals how much damage Tennent's image in the papers had sustained during the preceding twelve months: "We hear for certain, that the famous Mr. Gilbert Tennent has left his little Flock at Brunswick, and is gone to preach at Philadelphia, in the great House built there for Mr. Whitefield. It is reported, one Reason of his Removal was want of Success. And 'tis said he is become a meer Beau, since he married his rich Wife."[71]

Tennent did not vary his approach to public criticism in the years that followed. When his Philadelphia home was struck by lightning in the summer of 1745, the *Boston Gazette* (July 30) and the *Boston Weekly Newsletter* (August 1) reported the event, with the *News-letter* noting that Tennent "had both his Shoes tore off his Feet, the Corner of his Steel Shoe-Buckle melted, his right Foot wounded, his left one chang'd black, as was the upper Part of his right one." When the local Moravians interpreted this as God's warning to Tennent, Tennent preached and printed a sermon, *All Things Come Alike to All* (Philadelphia, 1745), to refute this rumor.[72]

When Whitefield returned to the colonies for his second preaching tour in October 1744, contributors to the papers warned readers of encouraging Whitefield in his return to the colonies, and Tennent's name occasionally appeared in the letters.[73] On February 18, 1746, a letter from Tennent appeared in the *Boston Gazette* defending himself against charges that he called ministers unconverted and encouraged church divisions and separations. Again, Tennent was strong in his defense, even turning the tables on his accusers: "I forgive the ungenerous Method that some Gentlemen your Way have taken to blacken my

Character, by printing the aforesaid Calumnies some Years after I was among you, who spoke not a Word about such Things to me while I was there, nor let me know any Thing about them 'till I saw them from the Press." The letter was dated November 8, 1745, from Philadelphia. Two contributors to the *Boston Evening-Post* responded by attacking Tennent, while the recipient of Tennent's letter offered two defenses in the *Boston Gazette*.[74] That was the last appearance by Tennent in the newspapers during the years of the religious events known as the Great Awakening. In December 1747, Tennent appeared in the *Philadelphia Journal* (December 22) and the *Philadelphia Gazette* (December 29) when he preached a sermon on the lawfulness of war, a testimony to his enduring recognition in the colonies.

JAMES DAVENPORT

The Rev. James Davenport was the only other revivalist to receive significant and steady coverage during the years of the Awakening. Coverage of Davenport was shorter-lived than even Tennent's and more localized, as seen in Figure 3.4, but it was inflammatory and consistent during a four-year period, and reports on Davenport appeared in papers in all regions of the colonies. Davenport appeared in the colonial newspapers during the years between Whitefield's visits to America—1741 through 1744. Although his time in the spotlight was relatively short, Davenport produced more turmoil in several years than did Gilbert Tennent in his entire career.

Davenport's image in the newspapers was different from both Whitefield's and Tennent's in that from the very beginning of his ministry, Davenport's persona was quite conflicted and unstable. Both Whitefield and Tennent began their publicized ministries in the colonies with fairly consistent public personas. Conversely, Davenport's initial image in the papers was inconsistent and much debated. Readers had a difficult time reconciling what appeared to be contradictory aspects of his life and ministry. Specifically, his impressive piety was often seen as being at odds with his extreme religious enthusiasm and inappropriate public actions. At the beginning of Davenport's ministry, readers were unable or unwilling to resolve the conflict.

Ultimately, Davenport's public persona was reconciled by readers, and the resolution happened quickly and decisively. Unlike both Whitefield's and Tennent's images in the papers, which adjusted gradually over time, Davenport's image transformed at once from being conflicted to being stable, but, unfortunately for Davenport, his stable image was not a positive one. Davenport swiftly became the icon of everything wrong with the revival—a sort of anti-Whitefield. This transition happened in every newspaper that reported on Davenport. Sometimes the transformation would happen between itinerant preaching trips to an area and sometimes halfway through a preaching tour. In each case, readers ultimately reconciled the conflict in Davenport's public image by making him into a two-dimensional representation of what many believed were the logical and dangerous consequences of the revival agenda and mindset.

James Davenport came from a long line of distinguished clergymen and became one of the youngest graduates of Yale College in 1732, where he was considered brilliant and gifted. He was settled as a Congregationalist minister in Southold, Long Island, in October 1738. Even before the revival, Davenport was known for his strong religious commitment and personal piety. Soon after his ordination, Davenport began examining his parishioners for signs of true conversion.

When Whitefield arrived in the colonies in the fall of 1739 and revivalist activities began increasing, Davenport became involved quickly, preaching itinerantly in nearby parishes in early 1740 with neighboring minister Jonathan Barber. Whitefield met Davenport in New York on May 2, 1740, and recorded in his journal that he was "agreeably refreshed in the evening with one, Mr. Davenport, whom God has lately highly honoured, by making use of his ministry for the conversion of many at the east end of Long Island. He is looked upon as an enthusiast and a madman by many of his reverend pharisaical brethren" (416-17). Whitefield's evaluation of Davenport's already developing public image highlights what would become a consistent comment regarding the Long Island minister—his personal piety and commitment to ministry appeared to be in conflict with his attacks on other ministers and embarrassing public actions. Early historian of the Awakening Joseph Tracy records that Davenport once addressed his congregation for twenty-four hours and declared he could determine the spiritual state of his parishioners, forbidding those he deemed unconverted from receiving communion.[75] Actions such as these gave him the reputation for religious enthusiasm, yet many claimed to be blessed by his ministry. Thus, before he even appeared in the papers, Davenport was busy creating a local public image, which perhaps accounts for how quickly his persona developed in the papers once he began receiving more widespread coverage.

Davenport's name first appeared in the *Pennsylvania Gazette* on June 12, 1740, with various Presbyterian ministers when he preached at the general session of the Philadelphia Synod. Before he left the region for Savannah on June 5, Whitefield had personally recommended Davenport and the others, thus allowing them to preach from his platform on Society Hill in his absence.[76] The *Gazette* report was reprinted by papers in Boston and South Carolina.[77] When Whitefield returned to the Middle Colonies in the fall of 1740, Davenport traveled and preached with him and other revivalists throughout New York and New Jersey before Whitefield left the colonies for England.[78]

In July 1741, several months after Tennent had ended his New England preaching tour, Davenport embarked on his own preaching circuit of Connecticut with fellow minister Benjamin Pomeroy from Hebron, Connecticut. The pair preached first in East Hampton, Connecticut, and then traveled along the Connecticut coast between New Haven and Stonington. By the end of the year, Davenport returned to his own parish for the winter.

Newspaper coverage of Davenport's first tour of Connecticut reveals his conflicted image in the papers from the beginning of his itinerant ministry. The first two letters to appear in the papers note the contradictory responses. In the *Boston Weekly Post-Boy* for August 10, 1741, a contributor from Stonington, Connecticut, noted that both the clergymen and the people of the area "had no small Expectation that by his coming, the Work of God which had of late revived among them, might be carried on," revealing Davenport's local reputation as a revivalist. The writer claimed Davenport preached three days to "large Assemblies," and then "departed the Place to like general Satisfaction and Joy as he came into it." Yet, the writer also remarked that Davenport's "Conduct in some Things was strange and unaccountable" and questioned Davenport's singing in public and judging other clergymen as unconverted. He noted that Davenport was "so full of Rancour and Invective against unconverted Ministers, pointing out the Parson of that Parish in which they met, that the People were greatly shocked and offended."

The second letter from Connecticut printed on September 28, 1741, in the *Post-Boy* also noted the contradictory reactions to Davenport's ministry:

> In general things appear in two very different and contrary Aspects, and Men are greatly divided in their Opinion. . . . On the one side these religious Commotions have produced a general Concern upon the Minds of Men, a Reformation from some Vices and Follies, and some seem to have passed thro' a saving Change; and so far all good Men rejoice. But on the other hand many things appear in a quite different and contrary Aspect. . . . [Some are filled] with a bitter, censorious and uncharitable Spirit against all such as have not experienced these Raptures, or that don't look upon them as Evidences of an extraordinary and miraculous Conversion.

The author remarked that Davenport "condemn'd almost all the Ministers" from Stonington to New Haven.[79] The letter was reprinted by the *South-Carolina Gazette* on January 2, 1742.

One week later on October 5, 1741, the Rev. Andrew Croswell of Groton, Connecticut, a strong supporter of revivalist activities, contributed a letter to the *Boston Weekly Post-Boy* defending Davenport. Croswell applauded Davenport's personal piety, claiming that "his chief Excellency consists, in his Faith, Love, and Joy in the Holy Ghost. God makes him so exceeding Glad with the light of his Countenance, that he can scarce speak without smiling. Sometimes so much of Heaven is let into his Soul, as is almost too much for weak Flesh and Blood to bear." In all, Davenport's first Connecticut preaching tour produced six negative letters to the papers and two letters of support. Generally, Davenport's piety and enthusiasm for religion were praised, while his actions were condemned as being censorious and inappropriate.

Davenport's conflicted image in the newspapers during his first Connecticut preaching tour reveals one of the major religious conflicts in the colonies in the 1740s: how can one understand individual religious experiences that lead to improved personal piety and religious fervor, but also produce actions that many consider injurious to other believers and the established church? Davenport's first Connecticut preaching tour launched discussion of these issues, but contributors at the time seemed unable to account for the disparity.

The inconsistencies in Davenport's public image were resolved in the newspapers during Davenport's second preaching tour of Connecticut. Davenport's own actions in the colony encouraged the resolution, although it was not in Davenport's favor. In May 1742, after spending the winter of 1741-1742 at home in Southold, Davenport arrived in Connecticut for his second tour, with Benjamin Pomeroy joining him some days later. Davenport's fiery preaching and unorthodox actions caused two laymen of the Ripton parish in Stratford, Connecticut, to file a complaint against both Davenport and Pomeroy for disturbing the peace. The General Assembly of Connecticut had just passed a law for the regulation of itinerant ministers in May 1742 (printed in the *Boston Gazette* on June 29), and so both Davenport and Pomeroy were arrested. Pomeroy was discharged and Davenport was expelled from the colony. On June 10, 1742, the *Boston Weekly News-Letter* reported that the General Assembly of Connecticut had judged Davenport as having a "natural tendency to disturb & destroy the Peace & Order of this Government" because he was "under the Influence of enthusiastical Impressions and Impulses, and thereby disturbed in the rational Faculties of his Mind."[80] The *Boston Evening-Post* (June 14), *Boston Weekly Post-Boy* (June 14), and *Pennsylvania Gazette* (July 1) also noted the judgment of the assembly.

Davenport's image in the newspapers had thus moved from instability to stability, and instead of being seen as a powerful preacher who performed some unaccountably strange actions, he was now viewed as a disturbed menace to society. That this transformation in the papers was accomplished so quickly was due to several factors. Certainly, Davenport's actions contrary to Connecticut law was the most significant reason. But the newspapers also were very willing to report on the controversy and to emphasize the drama of the incident. Davenport was accused of "filling every Place with Terror, Consternation and Confusion"; the governor was reported as placing thirty guards on Davenport; the sheriff was reported as being almost "mobbed" by Davenport's supporters; and Davenport was presented as publicly praying for his accusers, "Lord forgive them, for they know not what they do" as well as asking God to "come down and smite them."[81] In addition, readers who had debated Davenport's character publicly in the papers during his first tour were silent during his second tour. While Davenport's first tour of Connecticut produced eight letters in the papers, his second tour produced no letters. Instead, six news reports and two reprints appeared in the Boston papers detailing Davenport and Pomeroy's arrest and subsequent trial for disturbing the peace.[82] In the absence of reader opinion, Davenport's persona was determined in Connecticut by news reports instead of public debate. Also, Davenport's unwillingness to appear personally in the newspapers certainly helped him transition into a two-dimensional societal threat. No personal letters from Davenport appeared in the newspapers during the 1740s except a recantation in August 1744.

One could also argue that the transformation of Davenport's public image began before he even arrived in Connecticut for his second tour. Between Davenport's visits to the colony, the papers printed numerous reports of incidents that many readers would find alarming and would naturally link with Davenport. The papers reported on parishioners leaving clergymen Davenport had deemed unconverted as well as revivalist pastors re-baptizing children who had been originally baptized by these "unconverted" ministers. Both the *Boston Weekly News-Letter* (December 10, 1741) and the *Boston Evening-Post* (December 14, 1741) also linked Davenport's actions to the meeting of the associated ministers of Connecticut noted above that outlawed itinerant preaching. These reasons, then, may also account for the rapid shift in Davenport's image in the papers from being conflicted to being that of a dangerous religious extremist.

Boston Preaching Tour, Summer 1742

Several weeks after his deportation from Connecticut, Davenport traveled to Massachusetts for a preaching tour of the Boston area. Newspaper coverage of Davenport continued to be strong. His Boston tour produced three times as many items in the papers as did his second Connecticut tour and was reported throughout the colonies. In fact, Davenport's forty-five appearances in the newspapers during 1742 were twice the amount that Gilbert Tennent produced during either of his peak years of 1741 (23) and 1742 (22). Including reprints, which appeared throughout the colonies, Davenport's Boston tour produced thirty-six items in the newspapers.

Coverage of Davenport's Boston tour followed a similar pattern to coverage in Connecticut. Initially, readers were eager to debate Davenport's personality, actions, and ministry. However, after much debate and rancor, the papers turned to coverage that, like the papers during Davenport's second Connecticut tour, focused instead on reporting Davenport's legal troubles and branding him a menace.

Newspaper coverage of Davenport's time in Boston reveals several realities about Davenport's public persona at the beginning of his tour. First, he was recognized as a newsmaker. His arrival in Charlestown was noted on June 28, 1742, by the *Boston Evening-Post*. Not long after his arrival, the associated pastors of Boston and Charlestown met with him to determine his suitability to preach in their pulpits. The ministers recognized that they needed to make a statement regarding Davenport as public attention was directed his way. Like Davenport's early experiences in Connecticut, the judgment of the Boston ministers revealed Davenport's conflicted image—they concluded that Davenport was a "truly pious" man, but that they could not condone his propensity to act upon "sudden Impulses," his singing in the public streets, and his encouragement of lay preaching. The ministers therefore refused Davenport access to their pulpits. Their declaration was printed in the *Boston Evening-Post* and *Boston Weekly Post-Boy* on July 5, 1742. The declaration was reprinted throughout the colonies by the *American Weekly Mercury* (July 29), *Pennsylvania Gazette* (August 12), and *South-Carolina Gazette* (December 13).

Davenport's image in Boston was as inconsistent and contested as it had been initially in Connecticut. Just as the associated ministers could not reconcile Davenport's "truly pious" character with his unconventional actions, readers struggled in like manner. On July 1, 1742, the *Boston Weekly News-Letter* noted that Davenport had preached to "thousands of People of different Sentiments," acknowledging the "different Opinions of Persons about him." The *Boston Weekly Post-Boy* for July 5 printed a letter from the Rev. John Owen of Groton,

Connecticut, who asserted that he found Davenport to be "an eminent and dear Servant of Christ" when he met with him during Davenport's Connecticut tour. He encouraged the Boston ministers to open their pulpits to him. Fleet's *Boston Evening-Post* for the same date included a letter from a Boston gentleman to his friend in the country who criticized Davenport's sermons as "dull and heavy" and branded Davenport a "rank Enthusiast." The *Post* letter was reprinted by the *New-York Weekly Journal* on July 19. The Rev. Andrew Croswell of Connecticut, a consistent supporter of Davenport, criticized the declaration of the associated ministers and defended Davenport in his *Reply to the Declaration of a Number of the Associated Ministers in Boston and Charlestown, with Regard to the Rev. Mr. James Davenport and His Conduct* (Boston, 1742), which caused several responses in the Boston papers.[83] A Boston minister's letter to a friend in the country appeared in the *Boston Evening-Post* on August 2, 1742. In the letter, the minister complained that Davenport's preaching was "generally level'd against Opposers and unconverted Ministers," identifying his "whole Speech and Behaviour [as] discovering the Freaks of Madness, and Wilds of Enthusiasm." The writer even worried that the religious excitement of Davenport and his followers "is so red hot, that I verily believe they would make nothing to kill Opposers, and in so doing, think they did God Service."

By mid-August 1742, Boston readers chose the same resolution to Davenport's inconsistencies as Connecticut readers had a few months earlier. Newspaper reporting on Davenport turned, like it had in Connecticut, from debating his character and ministry to reporting on his legal troubles. Again, Davenport's actions led the way. He was arrested for "his irregular and unjustifiable Conduct, in censuring some of the Rev. Ministers among us, denouncing them unconverted, advising People to leave their Ministry &c. and occasioning great Disorder and Confusion, contrary to the publick Peace," as the *Boston Weekly Post-Boy* reported on August 23. The *Boston Evening-Post* also reported the arrest on August 23. Davenport refused bail, and a trial by the Grand Jury commenced on August 19. The primary charge against Davenport was his slander of the ministers of Boston, calling them "carnal and unconverted men."[84] Yet, even during his trial, Davenport's personal piety still affected some: on August 24, six Boston ministers sent a letter to the court, assuring the court that they forgave Davenport for his slandering of them and asking the justices to judge him with "all that Gentleness and Tenderness, which your Honours may judge consistent with Justice, and the publick Peace." The ministers' letter was printed by the *Boston Weekly News-Letter* on August 26. The *Boston Weekly Post-Boy* reported on the progress of the trial on August 30 as well as the earlier success of Davenport's preaching among the Nihantick Indians.

On September 2, 1742, the *Boston Weekly News-Letter* reported that the outcome of Davenport's trial in Boston was the declaration of *"Non Compos Mentis*, and therefore not Guilty." The *Boston Evening-Post* printed a summary of the trial on September 6, along with a notice that Davenport had continued preaching every day in private homes since his discharge from prison. The *Boston Weekly Post-Boy* printed a short report of the trial's outcome on September 6 as well. The *Boston Evening-Post* also printed two items defending ministers whom Davenport had attacked—Theophilus Pickering of Essex (September 6) and Joseph Sewall of the Old South Church in Boston (September 13).[85]

Davenport's arrest and trial in Boston were reported by the *Pennsylvania Gazette* and *American Weekly Mercury* in Philadelphia. The *Gazette* reprinted the account of Davenport's arrest from the *Boston Evening-Post* on September 2, while the *Mercury* reprinted the *Boston Weekly Post-Boy*'s version on the same date. The *Mercury* reprinted the Boston ministers' plea to the justices for mercy for Davenport from the *Boston Weekly News-Letter* on September 16, and both Philadelphia papers reprinted the *Boston Weekly Post-Boy*'s report on the progress of the trial.[86] On September 16, 1742, the *Mercury* reprinted the outcome of Davenport's trial from the *Boston Weekly News-Letter*, while the *Gazette* reprinted the report from the *Boston Evening-Post*. As winter began, Davenport returned to his own church in Southold and received from them a formal censure for neglecting his pastoral duties. Davenport's image would never again be debated in the newspapers. Like in Connecticut, a legal judgment against him had ended the discussion of his character and ministry.

One noteworthy aspect of the newspaper reporting on Davenport in both Connecticut and Massachusetts is the focus of the reporting. News items and contributed letters consistently remark on the physical aspects of Davenport's preaching and behavior. For example, in the August 10, 1741, *Boston Weekly Post-Boy*, a contributor reported on the "vehemence and boisterousness of his carrying on" in Connecticut. A letter in the *Boston Weekly Post-Boy* for October 5, 1741, reported that Davenport's unsolicited praying in an "unconverted" minister's house in Connecticut continued "in the midst of the greatest Noise, Confusion and Consternation." When Davenport was in Boston, a letter in the July 5, 1742, *Boston Evening-Post* noted Davenport's "violent straining of his Lungs" and "most Extravagant wreathings of his Body." This letter was reprinted by the *New-York Weekly Journal* on July 19. Another letter in the *Boston Evening-Post* on August 2, 1742, remarked that Davenport's "Gestures in preaching are Theatrical, his Voice Tumultuous." Even a supporter writing to the *Boston Weekly Post-Boy* on October 5, 1741, admitted that "there is a deal of Thunder as well as Lightning in his Preaching."

A lengthy letter in the *Boston Weekly News-Letter* on July 1, 1742, reported on Davenport's trial in Connecticut, devoting an entire paragraph to describing Davenport's physical appearance during the trial: "Nextly, view him at the barr of the assembly: his approach to which, his air and posture there; that inflexibility of body, that affectatious oblique reclining of the head, that elevation, or rather inversion of the eyes, that forced negligence and retirement of soul, and that uncouth shew, that motly mixture of pride and gravity wrought up to sullenness, is not easily to be described. In this Posture view him invariable as a statue, 'till the adjournment and withdrawing of the assembly that evening." After leaving the assembly, Davenport was reported by the contributor to have begun exhorting the assembly with a "vehement stentorian voice, and wild distortions of body." Davenport's body was so often the focus of reports on him in the newspapers that perhaps it is not surprising that the judgment of both the Connecticut Assembly and the Boston Grand Jury did not address Davenport's doctrinal beliefs or ministry practices specifically, but addressed his mental functioning. Perhaps the judgment of *non compos mentis* was the culmination of the public's focus on Davenport as a representation of the specifically physical extremes of revivalist activity.

The judgments against Davenport of mental instability in both Connecticut and Boston reveal perhaps an unwillingness on the part of the clergymen in those towns to confront the central issue of personal piety versus community life sparked by Davenport's ministry. The fact that the newspaper reports focused so strongly on Davenport's body and physical actions reveals that many readers were unable or unwilling to move beyond seeing Davenport as a two-dimensional representative of the frightening excesses of the movement. With no personal correspondence from Davenport in the papers, he did not have the personal connection to readers that Tennent did and thus had less of an opportunity to be seen as a three-dimensional person. He was more extreme in his enthusiasm than was Whitefield, and did not produce Whitefield's astonishing results. The legal judgments against him in Boston mark the demise of Davenport's public image.

Final Moments of Fame

Davenport appeared in the newspapers two additional times after his itinerant preaching tours, and his physical actions continued to be a focus of the newspapers. The first appearance occurred at the close of the winter of 1742-1743, six months after the end of his Boston preaching tour. In time, this action of Davenport's would come to be known as the most fanatical religious exploit of the 1740s. Invited by religious Separatists in New London, Connecticut, to assist them in organizing a church, Davenport arrived there on March 2, 1743. On March 6, based on impressions he received through dreams, Davenport denounced the temptations of worldly possessions and ordered his followers to collect for burning their wigs, jewelry, and fine clothing. Davenport himself threw his plush breeches into the pile. Davenport also created a pile of religious books with which he disagreed. Included in the pile were works written by highly esteemed clergymen such as Matthew Henry, Increase Mather, and Samuel Sewall, as well as works by revivalists such as Benjamin Colman of Boston and Jonathan Parsons of Lyme, Connecticut, in whose church Whitefield was eventually buried. Although the clothing was not burned, the bonfire of books lasted for two days.[87]

The *Boston Evening-Post* reported the event, printing three reports on the incident which included detailed lists of which books were burned by Davenport.[88] The *Boston Weekly Post-Boy* was the only other Boston paper to report the incident (March 28, 1743); the pro-revival *Boston Gazette* chose not to report the story. In Philadelphia, Franklin's *Pennsylvania Gazette* reprinted three items from the *Post*.[89] Interestingly, this incident sparked not only reports in the newspapers, but also rumors about Davenport. On March 28, the *Boston Weekly Post-Boy* printed a letter from New London which remarked that Davenport had allegedly admitted to another minister during the burning that "he was under the Influence of an evil Spirit, and that God had left Him." The *Boston Evening-Post* printed a letter on March 28, 1743, reporting that Davenport had recanted his "strange Opinions," calling them "Enthusiastical and Delusive." The *Boston Weekly News-Letter* reported on March 31 that a gentleman from Stonington, Connecticut, had reported that Davenport was dead, although another person from New London had claimed he was "alive, tho' in a anguishing Condition." The preponderance of rumors printed in the newspapers surrounding this event was a unique occurrence during the revival and may reveal how Davenport had captured the imagination of colonial readers. Readers were willing to believe almost anything of Davenport, and newspaper printers were willing to print it.

After the New London incident, Davenport's image in the news-papers appeared to be irredeemable. While Whitefield was able to achieve continued success in the colonies despite attacks on his public image, Davenport's persona could only be saved through complete capitulation. Perhaps Davenport recognized this truth, for after dismissal from his church in Southold, a protracted illness, and private discussions with two clergymen in Lebanon, Connecticut—his brother-in-law Eleazer Wheelock and Solomon Williams—Davenport publicly recanted. He published his retractions (Boston, 1744) as well as a letter to Jonathan Barber, his friend and partner on many of his itinerant trips, in which he repented of his role in the book-burning incident in New London (Philadelphia, 1744). The newspapers quickly picked up the story of Davenport's change of heart. The *Boston Evening-Post* printed Davenport's retractions on August 13, 1744; the *Boston Gazette*, to whom Davenport sent his letter directly, published Davenport's confession on August 14; and the *American Weekly Mercury* in Philadelphia reprinted Davenport's letter from the *Boston Evening-Post* on August 30.

In his apology, Davenport had to face directly the same question newspaper readers in both Boston and Connecticut had faced in regard to his ministry. How could he explain his improper actions in light of what many considered genuine personal piety and zeal for ministry? In addition, in the public mind, Davenport had become the unwitting representative of the dangerous extremes of the revival movement—how could he confess his errors as wrong and not damage the revival as a whole? During Davenport's Boston tour, a contributor to the *Boston Evening-Post* had linked Davenport's fanatical actions to "this whole political Machine of Whitefieldism" (June 9, 1743). Could Davenport undo some of the damage done to both his own reputation and the revival through his public confession?

Davenport began by confessing errors in two areas—actions that undermined ministerial authority and those that involved personal religious zeal that was employed inappropriately. In regard to the first, Davenport confessed three errors that challenged the authority of other ministers—denouncing certain clergymen as unconverted, urging separations from particular ministers, and encouraging lay exhorting. The next two errors Davenport confessed related to his personal religious enthusiasm—following individual impulses rather than the dictates of Scripture and singing in public streets.

In his attempt to reconcile his two types of errors with his personal piety and what he saw as the validity of the revival, Davenport made several choices. First, he placed his inappropriate actions outside the main work of the revival. He called his improper actions "Appendages to this glorious Work [that] are no essential Parts thereof, but of a different and contrary Nature and Tendency." Second, he labeled his enthusiasm "misguided Zeal," thus maintaining his reputation for religious fervor, but confessing that it was wrongly directed. Third, he noted physical problems such as a "long Fever," "cankry Humour," and a "disorder'd" leg at the time of the New London bonfire. Most importantly, Davenport remarked twice in his published confession that at times during his ministry he was influenced by a "false Spirit." When discussing the New London incident, Davenport noted that he was "under the powerful Influence of the false Spirit almost one whole Day together, and Part of several Days." In this way, he spiritualized his errors, placing the blame not on a lack of piety or intentional duplicity on his part, but on a deception of Satan. In fact, at the close of the letter, Davenport noted that those who would suppose that he was moved to confess by a "Desertion or Dulness and Deadness in Religion" would be wrong because instead he had recently enjoyed "a sweet Calm and Serenity of Soul and Rest in God, and sometimes with special and remarkable Refreshments of Soul." Thus, Davenport was able to confess his improper actions, yet maintain his image as one who was personally pious and intimate with God, thus reconciling the seeming contradiction in a way that differed significantly from the public denunciation that he was mad. Perhaps he was successful, for, despite his actions during the 1740s, Davenport went on to pastor churches in New Jersey and returned somewhat to favor, being selected moderator of the Synod of New York in 1754. After his recantation, he did not appear in the newspapers again regarding the revival.

Unlike Whitefield and Tennent, Davenport did not receive much "neutral" newspaper reporting on his travels and preaching. Instead, he endured mostly attacks on his character and reports of his unorthodox behavior and the opposition it caused. Like Whitefield, the private side of Davenport was rarely seen in the papers, for he did not respond in the newspapers as did Tennent, except for his public retractions.

All three men experienced the power of colonial newspapers to create and alter public images during the 1740s, and each revivalist watched his image shift, sometimes quite significantly, during his time in public ministry. Whitefield appeared the most often in the papers and for a longer time during the revival than did Tennent or Davenport. As an itinerant minister from England, Whitefield had sustained, personal contact with only a limited number of colonial Americans, and he did not contribute personal writings often to the newspapers. These factors are probably part of the reason he appeared in colonial newspapers early on as an icon rather than as a nuanced individual, and may also be why his persona became so conflicted and embattled after his first preaching tour. Knowing the power of the press, however, Whitefield worked to restore his image and had some success by the end of his second colonial preaching tour. Although Tennent's image in the newspapers was similar to Whitefield's initially, he soon received significant criticism and attack from contributors, perhaps due in part to his willingness to reveal himself personally in the newspapers. In addition, Tennent's position as a local clergyman did not allow him to escape to another continent when the colonial movement turned acrimonious. He personally experienced the controversy and animosity of the time between Whitefield's visits, and he played a public role in helping the movement define and defend itself, unlike Whitefield. His attempts in the papers to explain his involvement in the revival appear candid, direct, and ardent, as do his warnings about the direction of the movement, perhaps revealing his pastoral tendencies. Davenport's image, on the other hand, suffered not so much from what he said in the public press as from what he said and did in public life. Newspaper printers were quick to recount stories of Davenport's embarrassing exploits and to emphasize his more extreme statements. Very little neutral reporting on Davenport appeared in the papers; most letters regarding Davenport were quite derisive and unforgiving, which may be why Davenport's letter of apology reads as so intensely personal and frank, the first time newspaper readers saw the human side of the preacher. His image suffered more at the hands of the newspapers than did Whitefield's or Tennent's and was as two-dimensional as Whitefield's original public image. While Whitefield initially represented all that was positive and hopeful about the movement, Davenport represented all that was flawed and dangerous.

That all three men were able to continue in their ministries for the remainder of their lives is testament to the power of both time and effort in restoring one's public persona. While Whitefield used public means such as his preaching and writing to keep his place in the hearts of his listeners, Tennent and Davenport maintained a consistent ministry in their local regions. While Whitefield was able to best recover his image and remained in the public spotlight for his entire career, both Tennent and Davenport returned to the position of private citizen and carried on the remainder of their ministries successfully, away from the limelight.

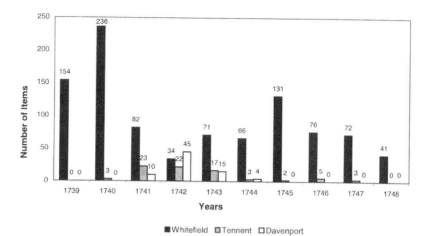

Figure 3.1. *Newspaper Items for Whitefield, Tennent, and Davenport*

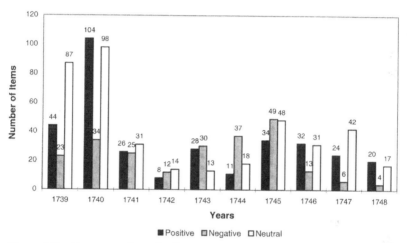

Figure 3.2. *Newspaper Items for George Whitefield*

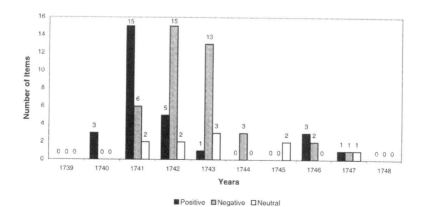

Figure 3.3. *Newspaper Items for Gilbert Tennent*

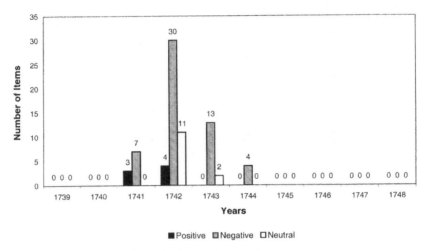

Figure 3.4. *Newspaper Items for James Davenport*

NOTES

1. *Virginia Gazette*, October 31, 1745.

2. Lambert, *Pedlar in Divinity*, 14.

3. Hugh Amory, "The New England Book Trade," in *The Colonial Book in the Atlantic World*, eds. Hugh Amory and David D. Hall, vol. 1, *A History of the Book in America*, 314-46 (Cambridge, MA: Cambridge University Press, 2000), 329.

4. This claim is based on the number of works by Whitefield identified by the North American Imprint Program (Amory, "New England Book Trade," 517).

5. Lambert, *Pedlar in Divinity*, 137.

6. Stout, *Divine Dramatist*, xiii.

7. See Lambert, *Pedlar in Divinity* and Stout, *Divine Dramatist*.

8. The lines are noted as being an echo of Dryden's verses on the frontispiece of Milton's *Paradise Lost*:

> Three Poets in three distant Places born,
> Greece, Italy, and England did adorn,
> The first in loftiness of Thought surpass'd,
> The next in Majesty, in both the last,
> The Force of Nature cou'd no further go,
> To make a third She join'd the former two.

9. In his journal, Whitefield admits to lying, swearing, and stealing as a young person. In fact, Whitefield recalls, "If I trace myself from cradle to

my manhood, I can see nothing in me but a fitness to be damned" (37-38). A recounting of one's early sins was an established convention of eighteenth-century spiritual autobiographies.

10. The concept of the New Birth was based on biblical verses such as John 3:3: "Jesus answered him, 'Truly, truly, I say to you, unless one is born again he cannot see the kingdom of God'" (ESV). One was expected to experience a sense of being born again when one committed one's life to God in faith.

11. See Stout, *Divine Dramatist*, 38-44, for an analysis of Whitefield's preaching.

12. Whitefield defended himself and his ministry in his journal: "I am, and profess myself, a member of the Church of England. I have received no pro-hibition from any of the Bishops; and having had no fault found by them with my life or doctrine, have the same general licence to preach which the rectors are willing to think sufficient for their curates; nor can any of them produce one instance of their having refused the assistance of a stranger clergyman, because he had not a written licence" (249).

13. The years between Whitefield's first two preaching tours, 1741-1743, produced slightly more than 20 percent of his total number of newspaper items.

14. The *Post* printed 139 items on Whitefield and the *Gazette* printed 215. Numbers for the *New England Weekly Journal* are counted in the total for the *Gazette* because Samuel Kneeland and Timothy Green, Jr., published both papers simultaneously, eventually incorporating the *Weekly Journal* into their *Boston Gazette*.

15. For Trapp, see *Boston Evening-Post*, August 20, 1739; for Stebbing, see *New England Weekly Journal*, November 13, 1739; and for Bishop of Gloucester, see *Boston Evening-Post*, November 19, 1739. For others, see *New England Weekly Journal*, July 24, 1739; *Virginia Gazette*, July 27, 1739; *Boston Evening-Post*, August 13, 1739; and *Boston Evening-Post*, November 2, 1739.

16. William Tennent founded the Log College in Warminster, Pennsyl-vania, and ultimately graduated eighteen Presbyterian revivalist preachers (Coalter, *Gilbert Tennent*, 5). See Maxson, *Awakening in the Middle Colonies*, 28-30, for a short discussion of the Log College and several of its more famous graduates. See also Thomas C. Pears, *Documentary History of William Ten-nent and the Log College* (Philadelphia, PA: Dept. of History, Presbyterian Historical Society of the Office of the General Assembly of the Presbyterian Church in the United States, 1940), and Alexander, *Biographical Sketches*. Theodore Frelinghuysen served as a minister in New Brunswick, New Jersey,

and greatly influenced William Tennent's oldest son, Gilbert, himself a Presbyterian minister in New Jersey.

17. Gerald F. Moran, "'Sinners Are Turned into Saints in Numbers': Puritanism and Revivalism in Colonial Connecticut," in *Belief and Behavior: Essays in the New Religious History*, eds. Philip R. VanderMeer and Robert P. Swierenga, 38-62 (New Brunswick, NJ: Rutgers University Press, 1991), 50-51. There are many valuable works which discuss the precursors of the religious events of the 1740s in the American colonies; see, for example, William McLoughlin, *Revivals, Awakenings, and Reform: An Essay on Religion and Social Change in America, 1607-1977* (Chicago, IL: University of Chicago Press, 1978); Gaustad, *Awakening in New England* ; Gewehr, *Awakening in Virginia*; and Martin E. Lodge, "The Crisis of the Churches in the Middle Colonies, 1720-1750," *The Pennsylvania Magazine of History and Biography* 95 (1971): 195-220.

18. Stout, *Divine Dramatist*, 89-90.

19. *Boston Evening-Post*, November 26, 1739; *Boston Gazette*, November 26, 1739; *New England Weekly Journal*, November 27, 1739; and *Boston Weekly News-Letter*, November 30, 1739.

20. Franklin Bowditch Dexter, *Biographical Sketches of the Graduates of Yale College with Annals of the College History*, 6 vols. (New York: H. Holt and Co., 1885-1912), 1:277. See also H. P. Thompson, *Into All Lands: The History of the Society for the Propagation of the Gospel in Foreign Parts, 1701-1950* (London: S. P. C. K., 1951), 38.

21. According to *American National Biography*, Smith "identif[ied] himself throughout his career with the radical Presbyterian faction in provincial litigation and politics." Smith worked often to limit the power of the governor and assisted in John Peter Zenger's trial for seditious libel. He refused the appointment as chief justice of New York in 1760, but served as an associate justice of the New York Supreme Court from 1763 until his death (9:352-53).

22. Besides Smith's original letter of November 26, 1739, letters regarding the controversy appeared in the *New-York Gazette* on January 22 (2) and January 289, 1740. Letters appeared in the *American Weekly Mercury* on November 29, 1739; December 6 and 20, 1739; and January 8 and 15 (3), 1740.

23. *American Weekly Mercury*, December 6, 1739.

24. *American Weekly Mercury*, February 5, 1740.

25. *New-York Gazette*, November 22, 1739.

26. "Philalethes" is derived from the Greek words "philos" and "alethes" and means "lover of truth."

27. Franklin's addition was reprinted by both the *Boston Evening-Post* (May 12, 1740) and the *New England Weekly Journal* (May 13, 1740). No

additional letters relating to the controversy were reprinted anywhere in the colonies.

28. This rebuke led to a short paper war between anonymous contributor Obadiah Plainman, who has been identified by J. A. Leo Lemay as Franklin, and Tom Trueman, whom Lemay identifies as Richard Peters, a former Anglican minister in Philadelphia. Plainman criticized the original author's use of the term "Better Sort," and Trueman defended the original author. See *Pennsylvania Gazette*, May 15, May 22, and May 29, 1740; *American Weekly Mercury*, May 22 and June 5, 1740. J. A. Leo Lemay, *The Canon of Benjamin Franklin, 1722-1776: New Attributions and Reconsiderations* (Newark: University of Delaware Press,1986), 98-99.

29. See, for example, a letter by A. B. in the November 10, 1740, issue of the *Boston Evening-Post* which questioned Whitefield's motives for preaching and accepting contributions as well as his encouragement of religious "Enthusiasm."

30. Of Whitefield's contributions to the papers during his first preaching tour, five items were reprinted entries from his journals, three were his published letters on English Archbishop Tillotson and slavery, one was a copy of a private conversation in England, one was a letter to a friend in England reporting on his orphanage, and three were reports to friends in the colonies with updates on his preaching tour. Whitefield did reveal personal details of his spiritual life in his published journals, but not in the colonial newspapers.

31. Three additional letters appeared on the topic; see the *South-Carolina Gazette*, August 23, September 26, and October 9, 1740.

32. *Boston Gazette*, June 22, 1741; *Boston Weekly Post-Boy*, June 22, 1741; *New England Weekly Journal*, June 23, 1741; and *South-Carolina Gazette*, July 23, 1741.

33. For a report on Mather's break with the Second Church in Boston, see the *Boston Evening-Post* or *Boston Weekly Post-Boy*, February 1, 1742.

34. See the *Boston Evening-Post*, March 14, 1743, for the first notice of the event.

35. See *Boston Gazette*, June 29, 1742, and the *Boston Evening-Post*, March 11, 1745.

36. The pro-revival testimony was titled *The Testimony of the Pastors of the Churches in the Province of the Massachusetts-Bay in New-England, at Their Annual Convention in Boston, May 25, 1743. Against Several Errors in Doctrine, and Disorders in Practice, Which Have of Late Obtained in Various Parts of the Land* (Boston, 1743).

37. *Boston Gazette*, January 11, 1743. Seven related articles continued the argument.

38. See *Boston Gazette*, May 24, 1743. The *Christian History* is discussed in chapter 2.

39. The author may be James Reid, a member of the Grand Jury of South Carolina. Evans 9496 also mentions a James Reid. However, the letter is dated "Philadelphia, June 6. 1743," so the author may have been living in Philadelphia.

40. "Publicola" probably refers to Publius Valerius Publicola (d. 499 BC), one of the first Republican statesmen of ancient Rome, who is discussed in Plutarch's *Life of Publicola*.

41. Publicola's letter was reprinted by the *Boston Evening-Post* on August 8 and the *American Weekly Mercury* on August 25.

42. Publicola's letters appeared in the *South-Carolina Gazette* on August 27, 1744, and November 19, 1744; a final letter was printed in the *Gazette* on February 17, 1746.

43. Whitefield long dealt with rumors that he was a secret agent for the Catholics. Jonathan Swift in his *Legacy to the Wicked Authors of the Present Age*, printed in Dublin and London in 1745, asserts the likelihood that the Methodists and George Whitefield are associated with the Roman Catholics: "I doubt not, but every Body in the Nation is now convinced, that the Reverend G[eorg]e W[hitefiel]d is hired and sent among us by the Queen of Spain; and furnished also with large Sums of Money by the King of France, to insinuate among the People, the Necessity of a thorough Reformation in Church and State." This excerpt was printed in the *Boston Evening-Post* on March 17, 1746.

44. See the September 24, 1740, entry in Whitefield's journals for his criticism of Harvard. Harvard produced a testimony against Whitefield in 1744, with Yale following suit in 1745.

45. On November 27, the *Boston Gazette* printed a defense of Whitefield in which the author called on the writer of the November 19 *Post* letter to provide evidence of his charge that Whitefield's teachings encouraged "Errors and Disorders." The writer asserted that Whitefield's followers distorted and misapplied his teachings. This letter was reprinted on March 11, 1745, by the *South-Carolina Gazette*.

46. *Boston Evening-Post*, January 7, 1745; *Boston Weekly News-Letter*, May 9, 1745; *Boston Evening-Post*, July 8, 1745.

47. Grasso, *Speaking Aristocracy*, 104.

48. *Pennsylvania Gazette*, July 31, 1746; *New-York Weekly Post-Boy*, August 4, 1746; *Boston Gazette*, August 5, 1746; *South-Carolina Gazette*, August 11, 1746.

49. See, for example, *Boston Gazette*, September 30, 1746; *New-York Weekly Post-Boy*, September 29, 1746; and *South-Carolina Gazette*, October 18 and December 8, 1746.

50. *Boston Evening Post*, February 4, 1745.

51. *Boston Gazette*, May 24, 1748.

52. See Coalter, *Gilbert Tennent*, for the best discussion of Gilbert Tennent's life and ministry.

53. Heimert and Miller, *Crisis and Consequences*, 80.

54. Heimert and Miller, *Crisis and Consequences*, 87.

55. For example, *Boston Weekly News-Letter*, October 28, 1742; *American Weekly Mercury*, February 23, 1744; and *Boston Evening-Post*, March 17, 1746.

56. Coalter, *Gilbert Tennent*, 72-74.

57. Tennent appeared in the papers four times before his New England tour: in a letter regarding the Whitefield/Arnold controversy (*American Weekly Mercury*, January 8, 1740), in a news item as having preached in New Brunswick while Whitefield was visiting there (*American Weekly Mercury*, May 1, 1740), in a letter from Whitefield (*American Weekly Mercury*, May 8, 1740), and in a news report as having preached in Philadelphia during the session of the Presbyterian Synod (*Pennsylvania Gazette*, June 12, 1740).

58. During 1739-1748, Tennent appeared the most often in the Philadelphia and Boston papers. The Philadelphia papers printed twenty-one items on Tennent during those years, while the Boston papers printed forty-nine. The *Virginia Gazette*, for which many issues are not extant, the *Maryland Gazette*, and the *Independent Advertiser* of Boston, printed no notices on Tennent, and the four New York papers printed a total of only two notices (*New-York Weekly Journal*, July 12, 1742, and the *New-York Weekly Post-Boy*, February 1, 1743). The *South-Carolina Gazette* printed two news reports and five letters regarding Tennent during those years.

59. One contributor offered excerpts from four different letters in the *South-Carolina Gazette* on June 18, 1741, so the number of items in that paper on Tennent is ten if one counts the excerpts separately.

60. See, for example, *Pennsylvania Gazette*, January 15 and February 19, 1741; *South-Carolina Gazette*, March 19, 1741.

61. The reference to "Boanerges" is from Mark 3:16-17: "He [Jesus] appointed the twelve [disciples]: Simon (to whom he gave the name Peter); James the son of Zebedee and John the brother of James (to whom he gave the name Boanerges, that is, Sons of Thunder)" (ESV).

62. See J. A. Leo Lemay, *A Calendar of American Poetry in the Colonial Newspapers and Magazines and in the Major English Magazines through 1765* (Worcester, MA: American Antiquarian Society, 1972), numbers 615, 616, and 617, for information on these poems.

63. All the letters discussed in this section originally appeared in the Middle Colonies and New England and were occasionally reprinted in the South.

64. See Coalter, *Gilbert Tennent*, chapter 4, for more detail.

65. See chapter 1 for Franklin's report in the *Gazette* and a short discussion. The Presbyterian factions were not reunited until 1758.

66. *Boston Evening-Post*, August 17, 1741.

67. In 1743, Tennent published *The Necessity of Holding Fast the Truth* (Boston), to which was appendixed *Some Account of the Principles of the Moravians*. See Craig D. Atwood, *Community of the Cross: Moravian Piety in Colonial Bethlehem* (University Park: The Pennsylvania State University Press, 2004), 39-40, for a limited discussion of Tennent's relationship with Zinzendorf.

68. *Boston Weekly News-Letter*, October 28; *Boston Evening-Post*, November 1.

69. The contribution in the *Boston Weekly News-Letter* for February 17 was reprinted by the *American Weekly Mercury* on March 24. See the *Boston Evening-Post* for April 4, May 16, and June 13, 1743, for comments about Tennent and the demise of the revival.

70. Coalter, *Gilbert Tennent*, 114-15, 122-23.

71. Tennent did evidence a marked change in his attire and preaching style when he began his pastorate in Philadelphia, abandoning his casual dress and extemporaneous preaching. Coalter suggests these changes reflected his new mission—to educate his parishioners on the more fundamental doctrinal truths of Christianity to produce a steadfast faith rather than to convert nonbelievers with simpler, hellfire-and-brimstone messages. Tennent's publications in 1744 and 1745 defended systematic theology and argued for Calvinist doctrine (Coalter, *Gilbert Tennent*, 121-24).

72. Coalter, *Gilbert Tennent*, 126.

73. See, for example, the *Boston Evening-Post*, October 29, 1744, and the *American Weekly Mercury*, November 8, 1744. Whitefield landed in Maine and preached his way to Boston, arriving on November 26, 1744, and remained in the area approximately nine months until August 1745, when he left for the Middle Colonies. Those nine months spent in and around Boston were contentious ones for Whitefield, as his arrival stirred up much of the controversy that had lain dormant during the preceding year.

74. See the *Boston Evening-Post*, March 17 and April 28, 1746, for the attacks; see the *Boston Gazette*, April 15 and May 27, 1746, for the defenses.

75. Tracy, *Great Awakening*, 233.

76. Coalter, *Gilbert Tennent*, 69.

77. For reprints, see the *Boston Gazette* (June 23), *Boston Weekly Post-Boy* (June 23), *New England Weekly Journal* (June 24), *Boston Weekly News-Letter* (June 26), and *South-Carolina Gazette* (July 25).

78. Tracy, *Great Awakening*, 235.

79. Perhaps in response to Davenport's actions in New Haven a few months earlier, Jonathan Edwards preached one of his most famous sermons, *The Distinguishing Marks of a Work of the Spirit of God*, on September 10, 1741, in New Haven. Kneeland and Green of Boston printed the sermon, which detailed Edwards' opinion of the characteristics of a true revival.

80. Historian of the Presbyterian church in America Richard Webster remarks in his work, *A History of the Presbyterian Church in America*, "The Patent-Office contains no specimen of Yankee ingenuity equal to that exhibited by that body [Connecticut General Assembly] in their devices and machinations to ruin [Davenport]." Webster, *History of the Presbyterian Church*, 538.

81. Excerpts are from two different reports in the June 7, 1742, *Boston Evening-Post*.

82. One reprint appeared in the *Pennsylvania Gazette* on July 1, 1742.

83. Croswell received a "faithful Rebuke" from an anonymous contributor to the *Boston Gazette* on August 10 for his vituperative attack on the associated ministers, but responded himself two weeks later in the *Boston Weekly Post-Boy* by denouncing the anonymous critic's rebuke as "a cowardly Attack made by one of the Devil's Soldiers" (August 23). Another opposer informed Croswell via the *Boston Evening-Post* on August 30 that his new translation of Virgil's *Aeneid* would feature Davenport as Sinon and Croswell as the Trojan Horse.

84. Tracy, *Great Awakening*, 247.

85. Few issues of the *Boston Gazette* are extant for 1742, so it is difficult to determine how the *Gazette* covered Davenport's Boston tour.

86. *Pennsylvania Gazette*, September 9; *American Weekly Mercury*, September 16.

87. Tracy, *Great Awakening*, 249; Harry S. Stout and Peter Onuf, "James Davenport and the Great Awakening in New London," *Journal of American History* 71 (1983): 556-57.

88. See the *Boston Evening-Post* for March 14, March 21, and April 11, 1743, for reports of the incident.

89. See the *Pennsylvania Gazette* for April 7, 1743, for three items. Another reprint of the same report appeared in the *Gazette* on May 26, 1743.

Conclusion

*[Some thought we] would not be so hasty and zealous in promoting
and maintaining the Religious Controversies of the present Day. . . .
And indeed with respect to us, they were not mistaken; for we
had some Thot's of wholly omitting them for several Reasons, but
chiefly because many think we have had eno' of them even to Sati-
ety, if not to nauciousness already.*

Jeremiah Gridley, publisher of *The American Magazine
and Historical Chronicle*, 1743[1]

Colonial newspapers were one of the chief disseminators of news and
commentary regarding the religious events of the 1740s, offering readers throughout the colonies timely, consistent reports on the progress
and perception of the movement. As such, they provided one record
of the religious events that would come to be known as the Great
Awakening.

In many respects, this record was consistent across the colonies,
offering readers one dominant picture of the revival and its various
transformations throughout the 1740s. Frequent reprintings and traveling preachers ensured that readers in all parts of the colonies would
read of the revival's main incidents and personalities. What is striking
about this written record of the movement, however, is the alterations
that occurred over time in how the papers presented the religious events
being reported. While the early years of the movement saw newspapers
in general emphasize the positive aspects of the Awakening, such as its
explosiveness, extensiveness, and power, reporting turned much more

negative after Whitefield's first preaching tour ended in 1741. Negative newspaper items outnumbered positive items for the first time in 1742, with the papers highlighting the controversy and divisiveness caused by the Awakening. In addition, contributed letters outnumbered news reports that year as well, and reader opinion continued to dominate newspaper coverage of the revival until 1745, when Whitefield was in the midst of his second preaching tour of the colonies.

The effects of the revival on colonial social order and religion were increasingly scrutinized as well in the papers after Whitefield's first tour, as contributors agonized over the possible consequences of the principles and practices of the movement. The integrity of the ministerial office was portrayed by contributors as being in imminent danger from itinerant preachers, while concerns over church splits and unorthodox doctrine provided the subject matter for many additional impassioned letters. Whitefield's reconciliation attempts at the start of his second colonial preaching tour helped turn the tide of newspaper reporting, with positive items outnumbering negative again by 1746. But reporting would never again reach the initial levels of support for the movement.

Despite a certain uniformity in reporting on the Awakening in general, the newspaper record of the revival did differ somewhat in each area of the colonies as local paper wars at times dominated regional reporting. Newspaper coverage in New England was the most frequent in the colonies and the most varied, with multiple Boston papers debating topics primarily related to religious tradition and stability. Anxiety over itinerant preaching and church separations provided fodder for many of the contributed letters, which were often scathing personal attacks on individuals. Yet, as opponents of the movement became more vocal in the papers over the years, supporters retreated, contributing virtually no defenses of the movement by the time of Whitefield's second preaching tour. Readers in Philadelphia experienced the second-most-frequent coverage in the colonies—coverage that tended to be more positive and news oriented than reporting in Boston. The authenticity and accuracy of the revival experience dominated Philadelphia disputes, where Whitefield and his cohorts received more public support. In New York, the lack of a strong revival tradition produced newspaper coverage that was in general limited, objective, and unoriginal, with the exception of James Parker's *New-York Weekly Post-Boy*. Parker's coverage was more extensive than that of any other New York paper, perhaps because of his partnership with Whitefield's official colonial printer, Benjamin Franklin.

In the Chesapeake colony of Maryland, reporting on the revival was limited, with Jonas Green's *Maryland Gazette* reporting little on the Awakening, conceivably because of Green's seeming lack of personal interest in the movement. In Virginia, another Franklin business partner, William Parks, used his *Virginia Gazette* to cover revival happenings closely, although a lack of extant copies of his *Gazette* makes a conclusive assessment of his coverage impossible. Lastly, in South Carolina, readers of the *South-Carolina Gazette* enjoyed frequent reporting on the Awakening as well as lengthy theological arguments on topics such as original sin, conducted by a dizzying number of contributors.

Leading revivalists personally experienced the power of the press as they watched their public images in the newspapers adjust, sometimes dramatically, over a period of months or years. Whitefield's initial image as the iconic, reverenced mouthpiece of the revival shifted to a more nuanced, fractured persona after his first preaching tour. His embattled image endured attacks as a dangerous divider of churches as well as support as a powerful evangelist in the spirit of the first-century apostles. Ultimately, he reworked his image to be more conciliatory and less threatening to the colonial religious establishment. New Jersey pastor Gilbert Tennent began his tenure in the public prints as a laudable "Son of Thunder," but later endured publication of his doubts and concerns regarding the movement. These hesitations damaged his position as one of the colonial leaders of the movement and a successor to Whitefield, and caused his persona in the papers to shift from that of an iconic leader like Whitefield to more of an imperfect individual, representing the flaws and doubts of the revival. James Davenport, on the other hand, managed to parlay several controversial preaching tours into a reign as the Awakening's "bad boy," appearing in the newspapers as unbalanced and dangerous in the extreme. In a matter of months, he became the representative of everything wrong with the revival. His printed recantation in the summer of 1744 attempted to both apologize for his errors and separate his extreme behavior from the revival as a whole, thereby preserving the integrity of the movement.

By the time Whitefield left the colonies after completing his second colonial preaching tour in March 1748, the colonial fervor surrounding religion had mostly subsided. The key players in the revival as well as the newspaper printers followed their separate paths. Whitefield returned to his London Tabernacle, and it became his base of operations for continued preaching tours. Spring and fall found him often in Scotland or, occasionally, Ireland or Wales, while he spent most winters and summers in and around London.[2] His preaching continued to draw crowds, and his friendship with Lady Selwyn, Countess of Huntingdon, created opportunities for a new ministry to the English upper class. Whitefield made four additional preaching tours of the colonies, dying in Newburyport, Massachusetts, on September 30, 1770. His funeral procession stretched more than one mile, and newspaper estimates of mourners ranged from 6,000 to 15,000.[3]

American revivalists continued their efforts beyond the 1740s as well, forming new congregations, increasing missionary work among the American Indians, and developing training schools for young ministers such as the College of New Jersey (later Princeton University) and the College of Rhode Island (later Brown University). Many of the revivalists became leaders in their denominations and worked to repair much of the division caused by the revival. In 1754, James Davenport was elected moderator of the New York Synod, while Gilbert Tennent was elected the first moderator of the reunited New York and Philadelphia synods in 1758.

Colonial newspapers continued to grow in both importance and numbers. By 1749, thirteen newspapers existed in the colonies; ten years later, the number had grown to nineteen. By 1765, twenty-six papers were publishing in America.[4] New papers sprang up in Portsmouth, New Hampshire; Newport, Rhode Island; Hartford, Connecticut; Woodbridge, New Jersey; and New Bern, North Carolina, to name a few, giving every colonist the opportunity to follow local as well as national and international happenings.

The content of the papers began to change as well, as new stories took the place of religious news. David A. Copeland in his study of colonial newspapers notes that news of American Indians increased by more than 300 percent from 1750 to 1755 as the French and Indian War and Cherokee War captured the public interest. England's hostilities with France and Spain also increasingly occupied newspaper space.

Slave revolts and slave crimes were other topics eagerly covered and reprinted by the press during the 1750s.[5] By the 1760s, political news began to take center stage in the colonial papers as America moved toward independence and expansion, with greater than 75 percent of newspaper space being devoted to politics by the outbreak of war in 1775.[6]

Scholars have long linked public discussion of the Awakening to later intercolonial incidents in American history, such as the Stamp Act and the Revolutionary War. Public debate of the revival made readers more comfortable with civic disagreement and helped create a sense of interrelatedness among the colonists.[7] Readers and printers recognized that newspapers could function as vehicles for transcolonial debate and as publicity machines for leading personalities.

The religious events of the 1740s offered colonial American newspaper printers their first intercolonial story. Papers presented frequent, consistent coverage of the events, personalities, and conflicts of the revival, while contributors submitted their opinions on the subjects that mattered to them. Newspaper printers and readers thus united to provide a unique record of the religious experiences of the colonists during the 1740s.

NOTES

1. *Boston Weekly News-Letter*, March 17, 1743.

2. Stout, *Divine Dramatist*, 207.

3. Stout, *Divine Dramatist*, 281; David A. Copeland, *Debating the Issues in Colonial Newspapers: Primary Documents on Events of the Period* (Westport, CT: Greenwood Press, 2000), 107.

4. Sloan and Williams, *Early American Press*, 103-5.

5. Copeland, *Colonial American Newspapers*, 273-74.

6. Copeland, *Colonial American Newspapers*, 269.

7. See Alan Heimert, *Religion and the American Mind: From the Great Awakening to the Revolution* (Cambridge, MA: Harvard University Press, 1966) for a discussion of how the Awakening influenced American public thought; more recently, see Michael Warner, *The Letters of the Republic: Publication and the Public Sphere in Eighteenth-Century America* (Cambridge, MA: Harvard University Press, 1990), 57; Copeland, *Colonial American Newspapers*, 274; and Lambert, *Pedlar in Divinity*, 170.

Appendix 1: Methodology

For this study of colonial American newspapers and the First Great Awakening, I examined microfilmed copies of the following newspapers for a ten-year period, 1739-1748: from Boston, the *Boston Evening-Post* (1739-1748, inclusive), *Boston Gazette* (1739-1748), *Boston Weekly News-Letter* (1739-1748), *Boston Weekly Post-Boy* (1739-1748), *Independent Advertiser* (1748), and *New England Weekly Journal* (1739-1741); from New York, the *New-York Evening-Post* (1744-1748), *New-York Gazette* (1739-1744), *New-York Weekly Journal* (1739-1748), and *New-York Weekly Post-Boy* (1743-1748);[1] from Philadelphia, the *American Weekly Mercury* (1739-1746), *Pennsylvania Gazette* (1739-1748), and *Pennsylvania Journal* (1742-1748); from Maryland, the *Maryland Gazette* (1745-1748); from Virginia, the *Virginia Gazette* (1739-1746); and from South Carolina, the *South-Carolina Gazette* (1739-1748). The years chosen coincide with George Whitefield's first (1739-1741) and second (1744-1748) preaching tours of the colonies. All news reports, contributed letters, poems, and excerpts from published writings relating to the Awakening or its participants were included in the study. General articles on religion and printing announcements of revival-related texts were not included.

I found 1598 items related to the revival and identified each item as "positive," "negative," or "neutral." Neutral items offered impartial information regarding the revival or its participants in an unbiased manner and were usually news reports. Positive items presented the revival or revivalists in an encouraging light, while negative items criticized or opposed the movement or included content that was disparaging to the revival or its participants.

When material is quoted directly from the newspapers, I changed colons at the ends of sentences in the original to periods, presented italicized text in normal font, and retained capital letters as they appear in the original. I also retained most eighteenth-century spelling variations.

NOTE

1. On January 12, 1747, the *New-York Weekly Post-Boy* became the *New-York Gazette, Revived in the Weekly Post-Boy* without a change in numbering. In my calculations, I included statistics for this *New-York Gazette* under the heading of *New-York Weekly Post-Boy*.

Appendix 2: Table of Individual Newspaper Reporting on the Revival

Table 1. Number of revival-related items printed in colonial newspapers, 1739-1748

	1739			1740			1741			1742			1743			1744		
	Positive[1]	Negative	Neutral	Positive	Negative	Neutral	Positive	Negative	Neutral	Positive	Negative	Neutral	Positive	Negative	Neutral	Positive	Negative	Neutral
American Weekly Mercury	10	1	11	21	4	15	2	3	5	4	14	3	1	9	5	0	12	0
Boston Evening-Post	3	10	7	5	11	3	2	4	1	4	57	11	1	50	9	1	41	6
Boston Gazette	1	2	9	2	0	3	6	7	4	9	3	1	11	3	13	9	1	4
Boston Weekly News-Letter	6	2	8	14	2	14	4	2	7	6	18	5	3	6	10	0	3	9
Boston Weekly Post-Boy	1	1	3	3	2	10	3	15	1	4	25	10	1	3	2	0	0	1
Independent Advertiser	n/a	n/a	n/a	n/a	n/a	n/a	n/a	n/a	n/a	n/a	n/a	n/a	n/a	n/a	n/a	n/a	n/a	n/a
Maryland Gazette	n/a	n/a	n/a	n/a	n/a	n/a	n/a	n/a	n/a	n/a	n/a	n/a	n/a	n/a	n/a	n/a	n/a	n/a
New England Weekly Journal	7	1	14	17	1	33	18	2	11	n/a	n/a	n/a	n/a	n/a	n/a	n/a	n/a	n/a
New-York Evening-Post	n/a	n/a	n/a	n/a	n/a	n/a	n/a	n/a	n/a	n/a	n/a	n/a	n/a	n/a	n/a	0	0	0
New-York Gazette	9	0	6	8	1	2	0	0	0	0	0	0	0	0	0	0	0	0
New-York Weekly Journal	5	4	7	0	4	4	5	3	4	2	10	1	2	4	3	0	0	1
New-York Weekly Post-Boy[2]	n/a	n/a	n/a	n/a	n/a	n/a	n/a	n/a	n/a	n/a	n/a	n/a	0	0	4	1	4	4
Pennsylvania Gazette	5	0	10	22	3	19	5	2	6	5	9	8	5	6	9	0	2	4
Pennsylvania Journal	n/a	n/a	n/a	n/a	n/a	n/a	n/a	n/a	n/a	0	0	1	8	0	4	2	0	3
South-Carolina Gazette	1	0	2	22	12	14	7	13	7	2	10	6	3	6	1	1	4	0
Virginia Gazette[3]	2	5	8	3	0	2	0	0	0	0	0	0	0	0	0	0	0	0

	1745			1746			1747			1748			Totals			
	Positive	Negative	Neutral	Positive	Negative	Neutral	Positive	Negative	Neutral	Positive	Negative	Neutral	Positive	Negative	Neutral	Grand Total
American Weekly Mercury	2	5	6	0	3	0	n/a	n/a	n/a	n/a	n/a	n/a	40	51	45	136
Boston Evening-Post	1	54	9	1	12	7	1	9	10	0	8	7	20	256	69	345
Boston Gazette	19	1	22	14	1	7	12	0	19	11	1	8	94	19	90	203
Boston Weekly News-Letter	0	6	2	0	0	2	0	0	4	0	1	2	33	40	63	136
Boston Weekly Post-Boy	0	0	0	0	0	2	0	0	0	0	1	0	12	47	29	88
Independent Advertiser	n/a	n/a	n/a	n/a	n/a	n/a	n/a	n/a	n/a	6	1	2	6	1	2	9
Maryland Gazette	0	0	1	0	1	1	0	2	2	0	0	0	0	3	4	7
New England Weekly Journal	n/a	n/a	n/a	n/a	n/a	n/a	n/a	n/a	n/a	n/a	n/a	n/a	42	4	58	104
New-York Evening-Post	1	0	2	1	2	0	0	0	2	0	1	3	2	3	7	12
New-York Gazette	n/a	n/a	n/a	n/a	n/a	n/a	n/a	n/a	n/a	n/a	n/a	n/a	17	1	8	26
New-York Weekly Journal	1	0	1	0	0	1	0	0	2	0	0	0	15	25	24	64
New-York Weekly Post-Boy	9	3	5	3	1	6	2	0	6	1	0	6	16	8	31	55
Pennsylvania Gazette	5	4	6	5	0	5	5	0	10	2	0	2	59	26	79	164
Pennsylvania Journal	3	0	7	9	1	12	5	1	14	3	0	3	30	2	44	76
South-Carolina Gazette	5	10	5	3	4	0	1	3	5	2	0	0	47	62	40	149
Virginia Gazette	1	1	2	0	0	0	0	0	0	0	0	0	6	6	12	24

NOTES

1. Numbers are listed as positive, negative, or neutral in terms of the tone of the newspaper item toward the revival and/or its participants.

2. On January 12, 1747, the *New-York Weekly Post-Boy* became the *New-York Gazette, Revived in the Weekly Post-Boy* without a change in numbering. In my calculations, I included statistics for this *New-York Gazette* under the heading of *New-York Weekly Post-Boy*.

3. There are not many extant copies of the *Virginia Gazette* for the years 1740-1744.

Bibliography

Alexander, Archibald. *Biographical Sketches of the Founder, and Principal Alumni of the Log College.* Princeton, NJ, 1845.

American National Biography. 24 vols. New York: Oxford University Press, 1999.

Amory, Hugh. "The New England Book Trade." In *The Colonial Book in the Atlantic World*, edited by Hugh Amory and David D. Hall. Vol. 1, *A History of the Book in America*, 314-46. Cambridge, MA: Cambridge University Press, 2000.

Amory, Hugh, and David D. Hall, eds., *The Colonial Book in the Atlantic World.* Vol. 1, *A History of the Book in America.* Cambridge, MA: Cambridge University Press, 2000.

Atwood, Craig D. *Community of the Cross: Moravian Piety in Colonial Bethlehem.* University Park: The Pennsylvania State University Press, 2004.

Baker, Ira L. "Elizabeth Timothy: America's First Woman Editor." *Journalism Quarterly* 54 (1977): 280-85.

Brown, Richard D. *Knowledge is Power: The Diffusion of Information in Early America, 1700-1865.* New York: Oxford University Press, 1989.

Bumsted, J. M. *The Great Awakening: The Beginnings of Evangelical Pietism in America.* Primary Sources in American History. Waltham, MA: Blaisdell Publishing Company, 1970.

Butler, Jon. "Enthusiasm Described and Decried: The Great Awakening as Interpretive Fiction." *The Journal of American History* 69 (1982): 305-25.

Clark, Charles E. "Part I. Early American Journalism: News and Opinion in the Popular Press." In *The Colonial Book in the Atlantic World*, edited by Hugh Amory and David D. Hall. Vol. 1, *A History of the Book in America*, 347-66. Cambridge, MA: Cambridge University Press, 2000.

––––––. *The Public Prints: The Newspaper in Anglo-American Culture, 1665-1740.* New York: Oxford University Press, 1994.

Coalter, Milton J., Jr. *Gilbert Tennent, Son of Thunder: A Case Study of Continental Pietism's Impact on the First Great Awakening in the Middle Colonies.* Contributions to the Study of Religion 18. New York: Greenwood Press, 1986.

Cohen, Hennig. *The South-Carolina Gazette, 1732-1775.* Columbia: University of South Carolina Press, 1953.

Conforti, Joseph A. *Jonathan Edwards, Religious Tradition and American Culture.* Chapel Hill: University of North Carolina Press, 1995.

Copeland, David A. *Colonial American Newspapers: Character and Content.* Newark: University of Delaware Press, 1997.

––––––. *Debating the Issues in Colonial Newspapers*: *Primary Documents on Events of the Period.* Westport, CT: Greenwood Press, 2000.

Crawford, Michael J. *Seasons of Grace: Colonial New England's Revival Tradition in Its British Context.* Oxford, England: Oxford University Press, 1991.

Dexter, Franklin Bowditch. *Biographical Sketches of the Graduates of Yale College with Annals of the College History.* 6 vols. New York: H. Holt and Co., 1885-1912.

Dictionary of National Biography: From the Earliest Times to 1900. 66 vols. in 22. London: Oxford University Press, 1921-1922.

Durden, Susan. "A Study of the First Evangelical Magazines, 1740-1748," *Journal of Ecclesiastical History* 27 (1976): 255-75.

Dyer, Alan. *A Biography of James Parker, Colonial Printer.* New York: Whitson Publishing Co., 1982.

Eberhard, Wallace B. "Press and Post Office in Eighteenth-Century America: Origins of a Public Policy." In *Newsletters to Newspapers*: *Eighteenth-Century Journalism.* Morgantown: The School of Journalism, West Virginia University, 1977.

Franklin, Benjamin. *The General Magazine and Historical Chronicle.* Vol. 1, no. 3. New York: Columbia University Press, 1938.

Gaustad, Edwin Scott. *The Great Awakening in New England.* New York: Harper & Brothers, 1957.

Gewehr, Wesley M. *The Great Awakening in Virginia, 1740-1790.* Durham, NC: Duke University Press, 1930.

Grasso, Christopher A. *Speaking Aristocracy: Transforming Public Discourse in Eighteenth-Century Connecticut.* Chapel Hill, NC: Omohundro Institute of Early American History and Culture and University of North Carolina Press, 1999.

Green, James N. "Part I. English Books and Printing in the Age of Franklin." In *The Colonial Book in the Atlantic World*, edited by Hugh Amory and David D. Hall. Vol. 1, *A History of the Book in America*, 248-98. Cambridge, MA: Cambridge University Press, 2000.

Hall, David D. "Part I. The Atlantic Economy in the Eighteenth Century." In *The Colonial Book in the Atlantic World*, edited by Hugh Amory and David D. Hall. Vol. 1, *A History of the Book in America*, 152-62. Cambridge, MA: Cambridge University Press, 2000.

Hambrick-Stowe, Charles E. "The Spirit of the Old Writers: Print Media, the Great Awakening, and Continuity in New England." In *Communication and Change in American Religious History*, edited by Leonard I. Sweet, 128-35. Grand Rapids, MI: Eerdmans, 1993.

Hamilton, Alexander. *The History of the Ancient and Honorable Tuesday Club*. Edited by Robert Micklus. 3 vols. Chapel Hill: University of North Carolina Press, 1990.

Heimert, Alan. *Religion and the American Mind: From the Great Awakening to the Revolution*. Cambridge, MA: Harvard University Press, 1966.

Heimert, Alan, and Perry Miller, eds. *The Great Awakening: Documents Illustrating the Crisis and Its Consequences*. American Heritage Series 34. New York: Bobbs-Merrill, 1967.

Jones, Barney L. "John Caldwell, Critic of the Great Awakening in New England." In *A Miscellany of American Christianity: Essays in Honor of H. Shelton Smith*, edited by Stuart C. Henry, 168-82. Durham, NC: Duke University Press, 1963.

Juster, Susan. *Disorderly Women: Sexual Politics and Evangelicalism in Revolutionary New England*. Ithaca, NY: Cornell University Press, 1994.

Katz, Stanley Nider, ed. *A Brief Narrative of the Case and Trial of John Peter Zenger, Printer of* The New-York Weekly Journal. John Harvard Library. Cambridge, MA: Harvard University Press, Belknap Press, 1972.

Kenney, William Howland, III. "Alexander Garden and George Whitefield: The Significance of Revivalism in South Carolina, 1738-1741." *South Carolina Historical Magazine* 71 (1970): 1-16.

Labaree, Leonard W., ed. *The Papers of Benjamin Franklin*. Vol. 2. New Haven, CT: Yale University Press, 1959.

Lambert, Frank. *Inventing the "Great Awakening."* Princeton, NJ: Princeton University Press, 1999.

———. *Pedlar in Divinity: George Whitefield and the Transatlantic Revivals, 1737-1770*. Princeton, NJ: Princeton University Press, 1994.

———. "Subscribing for Profits and Piety: The Friendship of Benjamin Franklin and George Whitefield." *The William and Mary Quarterly*, 3rd ser., 50 (1993): 529-54.

Lemay, J. A. Leo. *A Calendar of American Poetry in the Colonial Newspapers and Magazines and in the Major English Magazines through 1765*. Worcester, MA: American Antiquarian Society, 1972.

———. *The Canon of Benjamin Franklin, 1722-1776: New Attributions and Reconsiderations*. Newark: University of Delaware Press, 1986.

———. *Ebenezer Kinnersley, Franklin's Friend*. Philadelphia: University of Pennsylvania Press, 1964.

———. *The Life of Benjamin Franklin, Volume 1*. Philadelphia: University of Pennsylvania Press, 2006.

———. *The Life of Benjamin Franklin, Volume 2*. Philadelphia: University of Pennsylvania Press, 2006.

———. *Men of Letters in Colonial Maryland*. Knoxville: University of Tennessee Press, 1982.

Lemay, J. A. Leo, and P. M. Zall. *The Autobiography of Benjamin Franklin: A Genetic Text*. Knoxville: University of Tennessee Press, 1981.

Lodge, Martin E. "The Crisis of the Churches in the Middle Colonies, 1720-1750." *The Pennsylvania Magazine of History and Biography* 95 (1971): 195-220.

Lovejoy, David S. *Religious Enthusiasm and the Great Awakening*. American Historical Sources Series. Englewood Cliffs, NJ: Prentice-Hall, 1969.

———. *Religious Enthusiasm in the New World*. Cambridge, MA: Harvard University Press, 1985.

Maxson, Charles Hartshorn. *The Great Awakening in the Middle Colonies*. Chicago, IL: University of Chicago Press, 1920.

McCrady, Edward. *The History of South Carolina under the Royal Government, 1719-1776*. 1899. Reprint, New York: Russell & Russell-Atheneum, 1969.

McLoughlin, William. *Revivals, Awakenings, and Reform: An Essay on Religion and Social Change in America, 1607-1977*. Chicago, IL: University of Chicago Press, 1978.

Meyer, Jacob C. *Church and State in Massachusetts from 1740 to 1833: A Chapter in the History of the Development of Individual Freedom*. Cleveland, OH: Case Western Reserve University Press, 1930.

Moran, Gerald F. "'Sinners Are Turned into Saints in Numbers': Puritanism and Revivalism in Colonial Connecticut." In *Belief and Behavior: Essays in the New Religious History*, edited by Philip R. VanderMeer and Robert P. Swierenga, 38-62. New Brunswick, NJ: Rutgers University Press, 1991.

Mott, Frank Luther. *American Journalism, A History: 1690-1960*. 3rd ed. New York: Macmillan, 1962.

———. *A History of American Magazines, 1741-1850*. Vol. 1. New York: D. Appleton and Company, 1930.

Nelson, John K. *A Blessed Company: Parishes, Parsons, and Parishioners in Anglican Virginia, 1690-1776*. Chapel Hill: The University of North Carolina Press, 2001.

Olson, Alison. "The Zenger Case Revisited: Satire, Sedition and Political Debate in Eighteenth Century America." *Early American Literature* 35 (2000): 223-45.

Pears, Thomas C. *Documentary History of William Tennent and the Log College*. Philadelphia, PA: Dept. of History, Presbyterian Historical Society of the Office of the General Assembly of the Presbyterian Church in the United States, 1940.

Richardson, Lyon N. *A History of Early American Magazines, 1741-1789*. New York: Thomas Nelson and Sons, 1931.

Rutman, Darrett B. *The Great Awakening: Event and Exegesis*. New York: John Wiley & Sons, 1970.

Schilpp, Madelon Golden, and Sharon M. Murphy. *Great Women of the Press*. New Horizons in Journalism. Carbondale, IL: Southern Illinois University Press, 1983.

Schmidt, Leigh Eric. *Hearing Things: Religion, Illusion, and the American Enlightenment*. Cambridge, MA: Harvard University Press, 2000.

———. "'A Second and Glorious Reformation': The New Light Extremism of Andrew Croswell." *The William and Mary Quarterly*, 3rd ser., 43 (1986): 214-44.

Shipton, Clifford K. *Sibley's Harvard Graduates*. 14 vols. Boston, MA: Harvard University Press, 1933-1975.

Sloan, Wm. David, and Julie Hedgepeth Williams. *The Early American Press, 1690-1783*. The History of American Journalism 1. Westport, CT: Greenwood Press, 1994.

Smith, Jeffery A. "Impartiality and Revolutionary Ideology: Editorial Policies of the *South-Carolina Gazette*, 1732-1775." *Journal of Southern History* 49 (1983): 511-26.

Smith, Lisa Herb. "The First Great Awakening in American Newspapers, 1739-48." PhD diss., University of Delaware, 1998.

Sprague, William Buell. *Annals of the American Pulpit*. 9 vols. New York: R. Carter and Brothers, 1857-1869.

Stout, Harry S. *The Divine Dramatist: George Whitefield and the Rise of Modern Evangelicalism*. Library of Religious Biography. Grand Rapids, MI: Wm. B. Eerdmans, 1991.

Stout, Harry S., and Peter Onuf. "James Davenport and the Great Awakening in New London." *Journal of American History* 71 (1983): 556-78.

Thomas, Isaiah. *The History of Printing in America.* 1810. Reprint, Barre, MA: Imprint Society, 1970.

Thompson, H. P. *Into All Lands: The History of the Society for the Propagation of the Gospel in Foreign Parts, 1701-1950.* London: S. P. C. K., 1951.

Tracy, Joseph. *The Great Awakening: A History of the Revival of Religion in the Time of Edwards and Whitefield.* 1841. Reprint, New York: Arno Press, 1969.

Trinterud, Leonard J. *The Forming of an American Tradition: A Re-examination of Colonial Presbyterianism.* 1949. Reprint, Freeport, NY: Books for Libraries Press, 1970.

Tyerman, Luke. *The Life of the Rev. George Whitefield.* 2 vols. London: Hodder and Stoughton, 1876.

Walters, Kerry S. *Benjamin Franklin and His Gods.* Urbana, IL: University of Illinois Press, 1999.

Warner, Michael. *The Letters of the Republic: Publication and the Public Sphere in Eighteenth-Century America.* Cambridge, MA: Harvard University Press, 1990.

Webster, Richard. *A History of the Presbyterian Church in America.* Philadelphia, PA: Joseph M. Wilson, 1857.

Westerkamp, Marilyn J. "Enthusiastic Piety—From Scots-Irish Revivals to the Great Awakening." In *Belief and Behavior: Essays in the New Religious History,* edited by Philip R. Vandermeer and Robert P. Swierenga, 63-87. New Brunswick, NJ: Rutgers University Press, 1991.

Whitefield, George. *George Whitefield's Journals.* 6th ed. Carlisle, PA: Banner of Truth Trust, 1960.

Wroth, Lawrence C. *The Colonial Printer.* 1938. Reprint, New York: Dover, 1994.

———. *William Parks: Printer and Journalist of England and Colonial America.* Richmond, VA: Appeals Press, 1926.

Index

About the Author

Lisa Smith received a Ph.D. in early American literature from the University of Delaware, where she taught part-time for several years. Since 2006, she has been an adjunct faculty member in the English department of Pepperdine University in Malibu, California. Her current areas of teaching at Pepperdine include early American literature, literary study, and business writing. Her research interests include colonial American periodicals, revivalist literature, and religious writing. She has published in journals such as *American Periodicals.*